COMPANY MEN

A Wellness Guide for Black Men
in Corporate America

COMPANY MEN

A Wellness Guide for Black Men
in Corporate America

JUSTIN GRANT

This is a work of nonfiction.
**Company Men:
A Wellness Guide for Black Men in Corporate America**
Copyright © 2025 Justin Grant
companymen.org

All rights are reserved.
No part of this book may be used or reproduced in any manner whatsoever without the written permission of the copyright owner except for the use of quotations in book reviews.

ISBN: 978-1-959811-79-4 (Hardcover)
ISBN: 978-1-959811-63-3 (e-book)
Library of Congress Control Number: 2024919548

Cover Design: Awan Design
Interior Design: Amit Dey
Author Photo: Yasmeen Anderson
Editor: Marjorie Winful

Published in the United States by Wordeee, New York, New York 2024
Website: www.wordeee.com
X Formerly Twitter: wordeeeupdates
Facebook: facebook.com/wordeee/
e-mail: contact@wordeee.com

ADVANCE PRAISE

"Justin has delivered a must-read for every Black man who works in corporate America. Period."

—Ian Dunlap,
Founder, Red Panda Academy

"Through *Company Men*, Justin offers a valuable roadmap for Black men to maximize their leadership, and at the same time, embrace the trials and triumphs of corporate life. Every Black male professional— whether newly minted or seasoned veteran—should read this book and apply its lessons for longevity and success."

—Derek Dingle,
Chief Content Officer, Black Enterprise

"Getting a foot in the door with the world's leading corporations is just half the battle for Black talent. Building a lasting, rewarding, and enjoyable career is the ultimate goal. Through *Company Men,* Justin provides Black men with the blueprint."

—Frank Holland, Reporter, CNBC

"A deeply personal reflection on what matters for a group of men that truly matter. Justin leverages his storytelling ability to offer poignant observations and practical solutions."

—James Rhee
John H. Johnson Endowed Chair of Entrepreneurship,
Howard University, and author of *red helicopter*,
a national best seller.

"Building a corporate career can be a deeply enriching and rewarding experience. It can be a path to achieving your dreams and living the life that you ultimately want. As Black men, we have some unique hurdles to jump along the way, and *Company Men* is a tool that can benefit us no matter where we are on the corporate journey."

—Sekou Kaalund,
Executive Vice President and co-head of Consumer & Business Banking, US Bank

"Justin is a truth-teller—a trait that's made him an indispensable voice wherever he's worked. With this book, Justin articulates the challenges that so many Black men face in building rewarding careers. The strategies he suggests won't just help Black men survive in Corporate America, they'll help them thrive over the long-term."

—L.P. Green II,
Publisher, *Savoy Magazine*

"With a sense of great pride and devotion, I've curated my professional and personal training in lifting up the next generation of Black male leaders; you can say it's my calling. Without hesitation, *Company Men* is and will be an important tool that will enable our young people to be prepared, thrive, and sustain their careers in the corporate world."

—Aulston Taylor,
President & CEO, St. Augustine High School

"There is more opportunity for people of color now than ever before. At a time when the demand for talented Black men is at an all-time high, *Company Men* will be the fuel to help them capitalize on it."

—Forest Harper,
President & CEO, INROADS

DEDICATION

For Anika.

In loving memory of Juan A. Simpson.

FOREWORD

Alfred Edmond Jr.,
Senior Vice President, Executive Editor,
Black Enterprise

Almost everyone has heard the adage, "Health is wealth." Yet very few seriously consider how and why health, fitness, and longevity are necessary for wealth creation and long-term success. Our peak earning opportunities and marketplace value happen after the age of 50 or not at all. Whether it is one or the other is determined by how long we live, and how healthy and productive we can be over time. This is true when it comes to the time it takes to found and scale a start-up venture into a multimillion-dollar company or grow wealth over time by investing in the stock market. This correlation between health, longevity, and earning potential can also be readily applied to success in corporate America, where the average age of an S&P 500 CEO in 2021 was 56, according to the executive search firm Spencer Stuart.

Throughout my career as a media professional and senior executive at Black Enterprise, I've been privileged to interview and chronicle the journeys of many of the most significant and successful Black Americans of the past half-century. Included among them are iconic corporate trailblazers such as the late former AVIS Chairman and CEO Addison Barry Rand, the subject of my first cover story for *Black Enterprise* magazine, when he was named U.S. marketing group president at Xerox Corp. in 1987. However, as wondrous as it's been to help cover the career achievements of Black men like Rand (who passed away at age 74 in 2018 after an amazing career, including an impactful stint as Chairman and CEO of AARP), there is a tragic, parallel history of outstanding Black entrepreneurs and executives dying suddenly at the peak of their powers. A recent, still painful, example is the sudden passing of Kaiser Permanente CEO Bernard J. Tyson, a passionate advocate of racial justice and workplace diversity, in 2019.

Many factors contribute to the premature death of Black men in the C-suites of corporate America. However, one we can no longer ignore is the fact that too few Black men are healthy enough or live long enough to survive the arduous climb to CEO of a major corporation. It's hard to sustain a lucrative career when you're sick; even harder if you're dead. If we are serious about advancing the earning power and career achievements of Black men in corporate America and in life, we must recognize that maximizing our health, fitness, and longevity is about more than losing weight and building muscles. Our continued progress requires us to approach our health—mental and emotional as well as physical—with the same diligence, discipline, and focus as we would as elite athletes. It is in recognition of this reality that I am committed to total wellness and robust longevity in my own life, following a regimen of strength training to build and maintain muscle (I am a competitive natural bodybuilder), walking for cardiovascular fitness, good nutrition, weekly therapy sessions, and other lifestyle choices. I am determined to extend my marketplace value and my peak earning years (as of this writing, I'm 64, #Trainingfor65) by maximizing both my health span and my life span.

This is why *Company Men* is such a critical read for Black men who want to succeed in corporate America, especially those with C-suite ambitions. Its focus isn't just about how to make the most money or land the biggest job. *Company Men* is about equipping

Black men with insights to help us achieve physical, mental, and professional wellness while working in the pressurized world of corporate America. Although we continue to wrestle with the challenge of racial equity in our society, there has never been a better time than this present moment to be a talented person of color in the professional world. But there are distinct challenges that we, as Black men, must face to survive and thrive in this world. Far too many of us are dying during what should be our peak earning years. Many of us are struggling mentally with the grind. And far too many of us have been unable to convert our hard-earned wages into wealth. *Company Men* weaves together insights that will help Black men get ahead—with wellness across every aspect of corporate life as the ultimate goal and the truest measure of our success.

AUTHOR'S NOTE

Building a lasting and rewarding career in corporate America is difficult no matter what your racial or gender makeup happens to be. From navigating office politics to dealing with difficult bosses and co-workers, while managing the anxiety-inducing realities of layoffs and reorgs—all while working to secure your financial future—corporate life is not for the faint of heart. Juggling all these challenges while trying to maintain your health and sanity is a lot to bear on your own, which is why nearly twenty million self-help books aimed at corporate audiences are sold every year in the United States.[1] *Company Men: A Wellness Guide for Black Men in Corporate America,* is one of the few to speak directly to Black professional men, and address the unique challenges that we face in maintaining our well-being across various spectrums (mental, physical, social, and financial) while working in corporate America.

Most Black professional men, at one time or another, have heard some version of the cliché, "You're going to have to work twice as hard to go half as far," from well-meaning parents, teachers, mentors, and colleagues. The implication is that because you weren't born White, you don't have the luxury of just identifying your talents and passions to make a good living. You can't simply be the best version of yourself. You must be twice as good at whatever you do just to

---

[1] Source: InfoDocket: "Self-Help Book Sales are Rising Fast in the US According to New Data From NPD Group." Jan. 13, 2020

get a foot in the door. And once you're in, you must accept that even if you give your absolute best, you'll only be half as successful as your White peers.

For people from any historically marginalized racial group, this mindset is a pathway to burnout, cynicism, and a life sentence in a prison of perfectionism. But for Black men in particular, it is a mortal threat. Black men today have the second-lowest life expectancy of all racial groups in the United States, and climbing the socioeconomic ladder is not serving as the protective health mechanism for us that it does for others. In fact, the higher we climb the socioeconomic ladder, the greater the likelihood that we'll deal with anxiety and depression at some point, making us vulnerable to other life-shortening illnesses.[2]

After grappling with my own bouts of stress-induced illness and talking to brothers with experiences similar to mine, I felt inspired to write this book. *Company Men* seeks to counter the physical and mental breakdowns that can arise from the "twice as good" mentality. It also examines the unique pressures we face in attempting to fit into corporate environments where we still often find ourselves marginalized and underrepresented. To be a Black man in corporate America demands that you get comfortable being the only one in the room and that you're able to summon the will to press on when things don't go your way. Because they often won't. Isolation and exclusion are the shared experiences of many of us who have lived the corporate life.

Corporate America brings with it many advantages that make it an attractive pathway, including six-figure salaries, generous health benefits, and a path to retirement. If you're fortunate enough, you can do work that's intellectually satisfying while forging deep friendships along the way. *Company Men* is a tool to help Black men extract the benefits of working in corporate America while minimizing the

---

[2] I address this in further detail in chapter one.

effects of the challenges that come from being a person of color in these spaces.

We are fortunate to live in a time where we no longer need to be twice as good as the next person to get ahead. We just need to do good work, be strategic, and work to become the best versions of ourselves that we can be. *Company Men* provides a roadmap.

CONTENTS

Chapter 1: Surviving the Weathering Effect 1

Chapter 2: Avoiding the Angry Black Man Stereotype 23

Chapter 3: Building a Roadmap for Your Career 44

Chapter 4: Fitting into the Corporate Culture 65

Chapter 5: When to Stand on Your Convictions and When
to Let Go 85

Chapter 6: Adapt or Die—How to Survive an Ever-changing
Marketplace 99

Chapter 7: The Secrets to Networking the Right Way 118

Chapter 8: The Money Chapter: Understanding Your Worth,
Negotiating Salary, and Getting on a Path to
Generational Wealth 139

Chapter 9: Enduring the Dreaded Reorg (and Layoffs) and
Living to Tell About It 160

Chapter 10: Managing Thriver's Guilt 184

Chapter 11: Leaning into Faith 201

Acknowledgments 218

CHAPTER ONE

SURVIVING THE WEATHERING EFFECT

"He who has health has hope, and he who has hope has everything."

—Lao Tzu

On Sunday, December 29, 2002, Juan Simpson, a forty-eight-year-old senior executive at Ethicon Endo-Surgery Inc., Johnson & Johnson's surgical device maker, took his two teenage daughters to the company gym near their Cincinnati home for an afternoon of exercise and basketball. Simpson, my uncle, one of the few Black corporate leaders at his firm and in his industry, was in lonely and rarified, high-pressure air. Back then, 95 percent of all executive-level positions in corporate America were held by white men, and against all odds, Juan Simpson had managed to join their ranks. His role as Ethicon's CFO and Worldwide Vice President of Finance often kept him on the road, and the holidays provided a much-needed respite and a chance to spend quality time with family.

Uncle Juan was "the Man" in every sense of the word, and he was on the fast track toward one day rising from leading global finance at Ethicon all the way to the C-suite at its parent company. He was also a mean golfer, who was so good that occasionally, company leaders would invite him onto the corporate jet to fly to Ireland for golf trips, where they'd make friendly wagers and sip Hennessey from paper cups on the golf course. *Ebony* magazine even did a feature on him back in the early 1990s as part of a series on up-and-coming Black corporate leaders. Juan Simpson was blessed with a thousand-watt smile and bore such a strong resemblance to a young Denzel Washington that when the soon-to-be-famous actor asked my Aunt Graciela out for a date, she declined because he reminded her too much of her charismatic little brother.

"Juan loved his job," one of his close friends told me. "He never had a negative word to say about his time at Johnson & Johnson. He was respected. And he was the best at it."

On that fateful day in 2002, during a short game of three-on-three hoops with a group of his J&J colleagues, Uncle Juan complained of lightheadedness before collapsing suddenly on the court. A short while later, he was gone from us forever, dead from a heart ailment that had gone undetected during his annual executive physicals. His untimely passing is a wound from which I will never fully heal. And a health caution I will never ignore.

The Juan Simpson I remember was a lean, mean picture of health and raw athleticism. He was a gifted track star in high school and was so good at baseball that he was invited to tryouts with the New York Mets. When I was a teenager who possessed the physique of a string bean, he'd challenge me to do pushups until my arms burned. Uncle Juan maintained a professional athlete's build well into middle age. The way he lived and died brings to my mind the legend of John Henry, whose feats of strength made him a hero to his people before his heart gave out from the stress of his labor.

Perhaps most important for me, Juan Simpson was my beacon of hope for a bright future. I spent most of my childhood growing up in a single-parent home in pre-gentrified Brooklyn. My mother, two brothers, and I shared a two-bedroom walkup apartment in a modest Clinton Hill brownstone. We weren't poor by any stretch of the imagination, but we didn't have much in a material sense. Uncle Juan, my mom's younger brother, gave me a model for a way out. I didn't need to have a good jump shot, be able to run the forty-yard dash in less than 4.8 seconds, spit rhymes, or sling crack rock. All I had to do was hit the books and I could one day climb to the top of the corporate world and earn all the material comforts that come with it—just like he did. The house, the car, the clothes, topped off by a beautiful wife and a brood of cute kids. Hell, maybe even a chance to take a few flights on the corporate jet. Uncle Juan had grown up under the same humble circumstances that I did, so if he could make it, I knew for damn sure that I could too.

In the years since Uncle Juan's death, I've followed his blueprint and managed to carve out a career that's included executive roles at two of America's largest banks as well as a professorship and a seat on the board of trustees at one of the largest private universities in the country. I've gotten to this point in large part from lessons learned watching how Juan Simpson lived his life, but I draw equally important lessons from how he died. Since his passing more than twenty years ago, I've often reflected on how the stress of climbing the socioeconomic and corporate ladders as a Black man impacted Uncle Juan's health. I wonder about this because of my own experience grappling with the debilitating physical and mental effects of work-related stress, and because of my conversations with dozens of Black men whose stories mirror my own. Although the world may see us as threatening and physically imposing these stories—and Uncle Juan's early death—tell me just how fragile and vulnerable we as Black men truly are.

Today, Black men have the second-lowest life expectancy of all racial groups in the United States—with only American Indian/Alaska Native men living shorter lives.[3] And while research shows that

---

[3] KFF.org- "What is Driving Widening Racial Disparities in Life Expectancy?" May 23, 2023

education and higher socioeconomic status improve health outcomes for other groups, including Black women, the opposite holds true for Black men. In fact, the more successful we become, the greater the likelihood that we'll experience anxiety and depression, both of which often serve as triggers for negative health outcomes.[4] We know from medical research that Black Americans are at greater risk than their white peers for life-shortening conditions such as hypertension and heart disease, and for other stress-related ailments including various types of cancer, diabetes, circulatory problems, gastrointestinal disorders, and even the common cold. Stress kills, and there's no doubt that Black people are exposed to more of it on a continuous basis than any other racial group in the United States.

Additionally, there's a widespread and justifiable historical belief among Black Americans that we must work twice as hard as our white peers to only go half as far. I routinely hear this complaint from Black colleagues and industry peers, and it was a recurring theme in my conversations with the men I interviewed for this book. This is a burdensome, stressful way to experience life day after day that's not only due to a lack of representation in the office, but as we climb that ladder, it becomes harder for many of us to maintain the social ties with friends and loved ones we grew up with but can't take with us on the journey because they're on a different socioeconomic path.

Corporate America brings with it many advantages that make it an attractive pathway to a good life—six-figure salaries, generous health benefits, and a means to a comfortable retirement. If you're fortunate enough, you can do work that's intellectually satisfying while forging deep friendships along the way. But in exchange for these benefits come the potentially deadly stressors that may impact our bodies differently than our colleagues from other racial groups. Everyone who works in corporate America must become skilled in

---

[4] Washington Post- "For black men, higher education and incomes don't lower risks of depression, researchers say." July 25, 2020

the art and science of healthy stress management. It's part of the game. But for Black people, and Black men in particular, this is a matter of life and death.

Arline Geronimus, a public health researcher and professor at the University of Michigan's Population Studies Center, contends that the types of stressors that Black and other people of color must face in this country can erode their health over time in a process that she calls the "Weathering Effect."[5] Her theory is that chronic exposure to social, economic, and environmental stressors disproportionally affects the health of marginalized communities and Black people in particular. The cumulative effect of this stress leads to accelerated aging and earlier onset of chronic diseases. Geronimus likens the process of stress-induced weathering to a game of Jenga. Over time, piece by piece, the stressors of Black life can strip away at a person until one day they experience total physical collapse.

* * *

We're Holding On by a Thread

"It's unrelenting, brother."

—Christopher Harvell,
former Wall Street management consultant

Christopher Harvell represents the best of us as Black men, and I see shades of both Uncle Juan's and my stories in his journey. Like myself and other men I spoke with for this book, he has endured the physical and psychological damage of the Weathering Effect. Christopher grew up poor in Washington, D.C., in the early 1990s, back when it was still the murder capital of the United States. Despite his circumstances, Christopher was an academic prodigy who attended the historic Dunbar High School, the nation's first

---

[5] NPR -"Making the Case that Discrimination is Bad for Your Health." July 14, 2018

public high school for Black children. At Dunbar, he went on to become the first Black male valedictorian of a D.C. public school in twenty years. One of the most extraordinary things about Christopher is he was the rare Black male student that colleges recruited for his academic, not athletic, acumen. Seven schools offered him full academic scholarships.

But just two months after he graduated from high school, Christopher's life was nearly snatched away after he and his friends were the victims of a random act of gun violence. He was shot several times; one of his friends died from his injuries. Despite this, Christopher persevered. He attended George Washington University, and after graduating, he spent nearly a decade in management consulting on Wall Street and earned an MBA from Columbia Business School. He eventually left corporate America for good after teaming up with his wife to launch Dental Kidz, a pediatric dental practice in Newark, NJ.

Then Christopher's breakdown came. "I was in the ICU for three-and-a-half weeks, fighting for my life against extreme exhaustion which had caused a severe case of pneumonia," he recalled. "The doctors were pessimistic and my wife even started preparing our will. It was a terrifying time for us both." Christopher attributes that experience to his time as a management consultant, which, despite being incredibly lucrative, is one of the most stressful jobs in corporate America. Management consultants can work as many as eighty hours a week and are often on the road, which doesn't lend itself to a healthy balance of time for family, health management, and other personal self-care. It's a pressurized atmosphere, often with millions of dollars in client resources at stake. The profession is marked by high turnover, with 35 percent of management consultants leaving their positions in the first two years.[6]

---

[6] Zippia The Career Expert

"It was unrelenting," Christopher said of the stress of the consulting world. "My therapist explained to me that your body holds trauma, and I was holding onto a decade and a half of trauma that was slowly starting to release in a way that became unbearable." He credits therapy for helping him to find healing, and he's become a strong advocate for therapy for Black corporate men who work in high-stress environments. "I tell brothers all the time, if nothing else, it gives you an opportunity to be seen and heard."

We Can't Just Exercise It Away

Monk Inyang, the former lead marketing strategist at Anheuser-Busch InBev can relate to Christopher's experience, both in grinding his way up from materially humble circumstances and in dealing with the effects of intense work stress on both the body and mind. Monk, who grew up in Newark, NJ, found himself in the eye of a category 5 professional storm in 2023 after Bud Light partnered with transgender influencer Dylan Mulvaney for a social media promotional campaign. That project, which Monk's team worked on, sparked outrage among the brand's conservative consumers and prompted a widespread boycott of Budweiser beers and other brands led by the singer Kid Rock. This contributed to a 20 percent decline in the company's stock in the month following the campaign's launch, along with a more than $1 billion decline in sales. More than a year later, the company still hadn't fully recovered from the fallout.

The strain of that calamitous environment nearly cost Monk everything. Although he works out regularly and is in good shape for a man in his late thirties, Monk received some difficult news at a routine doctor's visit during the crisis. The doctor told him his blood pressure wasn't the same—that it was really bad. "You can't live with this blood pressure. We're probably going to have to put you on medication," she said. This was not Monk's first brush with job stress negatively affecting his health. Earlier in his career, Monk had worked as an equity research associate at a sell-side firm. A key part of his role was cranking out research notes after companies announced their quarterly earnings. "When a company is doing a quarterly release, you need to be in the office and in the chair at 6 a.m. to write the note. It has to be perfect, and it needs to go out in 30 minutes," he explained. "My personality is calm, cool, and collected, but this was my first time experiencing this kind of anxiety. I felt like throwing up. I was having sweats."

Monk got through it, but in his next role at Anheuser-Busch, he truly experienced what consistent, never-ending stress felt like. Not too long after the doctor's visit, Monk was laid off when Anheuser-Busch decided to downsize and restructure. The layoff turned out to be a blessing in disguise. Immediately after losing his job, Monk came down with the worst flu of his life, as if his body was purging the difficult conditions under which he had spent years working. But then a funny thing happened, which confirmed to Monk that all his health issues were tied directly to the unrelenting stress of his job. "My blood pressure normalized after being let go. I was surprised at how much my stress reduced." Reflecting on that stressful experience, he remembered turning to a damaging coping mechanism that's familiar to many of us: junk food as a source of comfort and relief. "I'd have this crazy week and just be like, 'You know what, I'm gonna have some fast food," he said. "You go through all that stress and your body wants to have some type of comfort."

Feeling the urge to indulge in unhealthy eating habits as a response to a stressful day or week at work isn't a personal failing by any means. It's a sign of our humanity. A 2017 study by scientists at Michigan State noted that stress during the workday can lead to overeating and unhealthy food choices at dinner time.[7] In studies of 235 workers based in China—including information-technology

---

[7] Science News Daily - "Eating your feelings? The link between job stress, junk food and sleep." June 22, 2017

employees who experienced stressful and high workloads, as well as call center employees who endured hours of rude and demanding customers—unhealthy eating became a go-to coping mechanism. Chu-Hsiang "Daisy" Chang, a professor of psychology at Michigan State University (MSU) and co-author of the study, observed that employees under strain "tend to bring their negative feelings from the workplace to the dinner table, as manifested in eating more than usual and opting more for junk food instead of healthy food."

For professional Black men, who are already at a higher risk than the broader population for high blood pressure and type-2 diabetes, this is a potentially deadly stress-relief mechanism over the long term.

Bad Habits and Rude Awakenings

One morning in early March 2021, my wife, Anika, handed me her cell phone as I sat at our dining room table drinking coffee and reading the news on my laptop. When I pressed the phone to my ear, a woman's voice pleasantly said, "This is Summit Medical Group. Would you like to schedule an appointment?" Anika had been pestering me for months to schedule a physical, and I routinely gave her the brush-off. I had skipped my annual checkup the year before, and my previous doctor retired during the pandemic. After doing some research, Anika found a doctor online through Summit Medical Group who she thought I'd mesh with after reading his profile.

Coincidentally, Anika gave me this nudge to address my health—which I felt was perfectly fine—during one of the roughest periods of my adult life. We were taking care of our third child, a newborn; meanwhile, my father, who lived 2,000 miles away, was about eight weeks away from dying of stage-four lung cancer. I was juggling his healthcare from far away as best I could, and in those days before the COVID-19 vaccine, deciding when it'd be safe for me to fly and visit him was a difficult and complex decision. Anika and I were also juggling the needs of our nine-year-old and five-year-old, who were forced to attend classes remotely at home. On top of all that, my job as vice president of corporate communications for a systemically important U.S. bank was relentless. The company lurched from one major initiative to the next, with a few PR crises mixed in between. It felt like I never had a moment to stop and take a breath.

As the stresses of corporate and family life were grinding away at me, there was simply nowhere to go. Visits with friends and family were a matter of life and death. It was a lonely time. To cope, I denied myself nothing when it came to junk food. I was always on the slimmer side and ran three miles at least four times a week. I figured I could get away with indulging in my fair share of cheat meals. I was crushing the hills of central New Jersey with no problem during my jogging sessions and was always pleased with my running times, so surely, I was a specimen of good health. My go-to fast-food chains during the pandemic were Shake Shack, Krispy Kreme, and Wingstop, along with my routine orders to our local bagel shop, pizza place, and sandwich shop. My philosophy at the time was to eat what I wanted and burn it off later through exercise. During the pandemic, when you couldn't go anywhere, figuring out which fast-food place to order from and waiting with hungry anticipation for the Uber Eats driver to show up was considered entertainment.

But despite my best attempts at staying fit by running a minimum of twelve miles a week, I was developing a bit of a squishy dad bod, which I chalked up to turning forty the previous year. It was simply my "grown man" weight, I told myself. I'd developed a stubborn roll of blubber around my midsection, my face had grown chunky, and, in a pandemic-era group photo with friends from a local biking group, I swore it looked like I'd even packed on a few pounds in the buttocks. When I had my blood work done ahead of the checkup, nothing could have prepared me for the rude awakening of those test results. One by one, I got the email notifications. Ironically, the first message about my blood sugar came as I sat in a Dunkin Donuts drive-thru line waiting for my turkey sausage, egg, and cheese breakfast sandwich. My blood sugar? It was elevated and I was diagnosed as a prediabetic. This meant that my odds of developing Type-2 diabetes within the next decade were high. I found this surprising because I didn't think I overindulged in sweets. My LDL (the bad cholesterol) was high, some twenty points above the optimal range. I was also severely dehydrated.

When I went in for the physical exam, my doctor confirmed I also had pre-hypertension. Although he assured me that I was still a healthy dude, my body was flashing all sorts of warning signals. I was like a car whose check engine, brake fluid, and transmission lights were on. The good news, he assured me, was that I didn't yet need medication; they'd caught my health issues early enough that I could reverse them through simple dietary and lifestyle changes. "You can't outrun a bad diet," the doctor warned as I prepared to leave his office. Instead of writing me a prescription for a statin or diuretic to get my cholesterol and blood pressure down to healthier levels, the doctor gave me a list of films to watch, including *Forks Over Knives,*[8] *The Game Changers,*[9] and *Blue Zones,*[10] plus a few books to read, including *Undo It!* [11] and *Eat to Live.*[12] After consuming all that material, I was to follow the recommendations made in them, then come back in three months for follow-up tests. Each of those films and books advocates the adoption of a whole-food, plant-based diet,[13] less consumption of red meats and animal fats, ceasing

---

[8] Forks Over Knives documentary: https://www.forksoverknives.com/the-film/
[9] Game Changers films: https://gamechangersmovie.com
[10] Blue Zones film: https://www.bluezones.com/documentary/
[11] Ornish.com
[12] Eat to Live: https://shop.drfuhrman.com/eat-to-live-paperback/
[13] Harvard Health Blog - "What is a plant-based diet and why should you try it?" March 28, 2024

consumption of man-made, ultra-processed foods,[14] and consistent bodily movement throughout the day. The doctor was sending me a clear message.

Breaking Free of the Pleasure Trap

As human beings, we've been wired by nature to seek out sources of pleasure and to avoid pain at all costs. This makes it easier for us to fall into some of the most dangerous traps that modern life has to offer, such as consuming unhealthy foods and leading sedentary lifestyles. Corporate life—characterized by high workloads, tight deadlines, political gamesmanship, and the expectation of always being "on-call" thanks to texts, emails, and instant messages—has created a perpetual state of being in a rush. All this makes it easier to neglect the maintenance of our physical and mental well-being. Further compounding the challenge of this lifestyle is sitting at a desk for most of our days, which heightens the risk of all the health problems cited earlier in this chapter.

In their 2018 book, *The Pleasure Trap*, Dr. Douglas Lisle, and Dr. Alan Goldhamer argue that our biological drives for food, sex, and social interaction are essential for survival but have been hijacked by modern conveniences. Our easy access to processed foods that are high in sugar, fat, and salt is particularly problematic, they say because they overstimulate our brain's pleasure centers and can make us addicted to them over time. Like my friend Monk, and millions of Americans across the country, this addiction had set me on a path towards losing my good health earlier than nature intended.

Fortunately, there was a playbook for me to follow to get my health back in check. In the weeks after my physical, I found myself a nutritionist and sent her my lab results. "Don't worry, all of this is fixable," she assured me. "We'll get your numbers right in three

---

[14] Yale Medicine - "Ultraprocessed Foods: Are They Bad for You?" July 10, 2024

months. Trust me." She helped me devise a dietary game plan and recommended I download the *Lose It!* app, which enabled me to track my daily consumption of proteins, carbs, fats, sodium, fiber, and other key nutrients. I eliminated most added sugars from my diet, instead choosing to get sugar from healthier sources like fruit while increasing my fiber intake. I couldn't envision ever going full-on vegan, so instead I opted for a diet anchored on leafy greens, beans, and legumes, plus fatty, wild-caught fish, seeds, and berries while cutting back on fried foods. You've still got to live a little—so I indulged in the occasional cheat meal. But in the weeks and months after that physical, I course-corrected my diet.

Beyond changing my eating habits, I started putting myself first when it came to managing my considerable professional demands by blocking off the first hour of every day in my Outlook calendar for moderate-intensity exercise. Through my research, I learned that I couldn't reverse prediabetes with dietary changes alone. 150 minutes a week of exercise had to be part of the equation, with a consistent routine that included a mix of strength training and aerobic activity. Consistently doing both would improve how my body stores and uses glucose, while improving my stamina, heart health, and cholesterol. By my count, this was a simple equation. I just needed to spend a little under 40 minutes in the gym at least four times a week.

As the months went by and I remained committed to my new regimen, I found that I'd lost the cravings for all the unhealthy foods that were endangering my health. I looked in the mirror and saw a guy who was starting to lean out. I lost 10 pounds and was even developing abs. In an encouraging sign the week before my follow-up appointment, one of the kids I coached on the local baseball team said I reminded him of the NBA player Mikal Bridges, who is 17 years my junior. That same week, at a gala hosted by a retired NFL player, someone mistook me for former New Orleans Saints wide receiver Marques Colston.

Despite those encouraging compliments, I was so nervous ahead of my three-month follow-up appointment that I didn't look at the results of my bloodwork when the email notifications came in. Instead, I chose to wait and find out at the checkup. I needed to know that all these changes that I'd made to my lifestyle were making a difference.

"What did you give up?" the doctor asked me with a smile after I sat down in the examination room. "Your LDL is down 58 points. And you're no longer prediabetic. Everything looks great, man. I'll see you next year. Just keep doing the work." I left that appointment feeling a sense of triumph and I'm thankful to my wife for harassing me about going to the doctor. The stresses of my job and personal life didn't magically disappear after that appointment, but my approach towards dealing with them no longer involved turning to sources of comfort that would surely kill me over time.

But even as I'd found a new baseline for maintaining the health factors that were within my control, the question of why I and so many Black professional men I encountered over the years were struggling with how to manage the stresses of corporate life continued to gnaw at me.

Flying High With No Safety Net

Monk described his experience to me from his days as a sell-side equity research associate. Feeling so much pressure from his work, he would sometimes break out in sweats and feel nauseous. On days off he'd fall into a dark hole of dread. I could relate as it triggered a personal flashback. I faced similar struggles in my first post-college job as a stock market reporter for Thomson Reuters.

During my two-and-a-half years there, the stress from the job caused me to develop gastroesophageal reflux disease (GERD), a condition in which stomach acid repeatedly flows into the tube that connects the mouth and stomach. GERD is a wicked and energy-draining condition that would sometimes cause me to vomit stomach acid in the mornings before I went into the office. Those types of mornings were the worst because they'd sap me of energy at the very moment I needed to be at my best and would prevent me from bringing the best version of myself into the office.

But while my job in covering news about financial markets as it unfolded in real-time was inherently stressful, I don't believe the work itself was the root cause of why the pressure I was feeling manifested itself in this debilitating way. There were other factors at play.

I began my career shortly before the global financial crisis of 2008 began, and as that historic market collapse unfolded millions of Americans lost their jobs and saw the lives they worked so hard to build upended. An intense fear developed within me that I could easily be next. The news industry itself was at the dawn of a massive shift that would eventually lead to mass layoffs, and at the root of my fear was the idea that I might one day find myself out of work. Despite all the hard work I'd put in, I saw an easy path right back to square one with no generational safety net to fall back on. But in conducting research for this book, it was comforting to discover that I wasn't alone in feeling this sense of anxiety early on in my career. Many of us are buckling under the heavy weight that comes with middle-class life in America, where debt burdens, the high cost of living, and limited social support cast long, dark shadows over the bright futures we've worked so hard to build.

"There are these mental strains and sometimes you can't exercise that away," says James Ward, a corporate architect and lecturer at Columbia University's School of Professional Studies.

Monk agrees, adding: "You're in this process of being farther ahead in corporate America than the generation before you. And there's this stress of like, 'Man, I NEED this. And not only do I need this—I need MORE actually."

Fortunately, there was a happy ending for me with the Reuters chapter of my career. I hung in there for more than two years, did some solid work, and made myself attractive enough to the marketplace that I was able to navigate my way into roles that better suited my temperament and emotional makeup. And my GERD condition almost miraculously disappeared after I had the good fortune to meet my future wife at a Brooklyn house party in my final year at Reuters. Her presence in my life gave me something more important to focus on, which eased my professional anxiety.

I will forever be haunted by the questions of why my superstar uncle died so young and the role the corporate lifestyle might have played in it however, after surviving and thriving in a corporate career that's spanned nearly two decades so far, I believe I have some answers and a remedy. I've devised a seven-part system for managing the stressors that will put your health and life at risk over the long term if you're not careful.

Conclusion: 7 Tips for Surviving the Weathering Effect

1. Sleep well, my brother

> *"Finish each day before you begin the next and interpose a solid wall of sleep between the two."*
>
> —Ralph Waldo Emerson

Although a stressful workday may drive us to want to indulge in overeating and junk food, there's a simple hack that can help you keep your diet on track: consistently getting the right amount of sleep. In the 2017 study highlighting the link between work stress and bad eating, MSU professor Daisy Chang says that a good night's sleep can serve as a protective factor between job stress and unhealthy eating. "When workers slept better the night before, they tended to eat better when they experienced stress the next day," she wrote. Prioritize getting enough sleep. It can make all the difference in the world for your health and wellness.

2. Nourish your body with the right food

"Eat your food as your medicines. Otherwise, you have to eat your medicines as food."

—Steve Jobs

One of the most ironic things about the standard American diet is its acronym: SAD, a diet today for far too many Americans. Excessively high in calories, sodium, added sugars, unhealthy saturated fats, and refined carbohydrates with low nutrient values, the SAD diet, is marked by large portion sizes and is low in fresh fruits, vegetables, and fiber. It can lead to deficiencies in essential vitamins and minerals while increasing the risk of chronic illnesses like heart disease and Type 2 diabetes. The prevalence of this diet has led to an epidemic of obesity as well as rising rates of cancer in the United States. Black men, as we've noted throughout this chapter are at high risk for developing each of these conditions and have the second-lowest life expectancy of all demographic groups in the country. Putting the right foods on our plates is a key to reversing these distressing statistics.

3. Find a job you genuinely enjoy

I will always look back fondly on my time at Thomson Reuters. Despite my stressors, that place served as my foundational career experience, pushed me to become a better writer, and prepared me for the professional world. But the role was so difficult for me that every job since then has felt easy. Eventually, I navigated my way onto a career path that better aligns with me mentally and physically. We only get one opportunity to walk through this journey of life on earth, and filling our days with work we enjoy and that brings purpose into our lives is one of the greatest gifts we can ever find. If you're tethered to a job you don't like, get out. Enduring a job you dislike is a special kind of hell that will zap your happiness and damage your well-being over time. And besides, life is too short for that.

4. Find the right doctor

In an alarming study from 2011, researchers from the University of Michigan found that a majority of Black men don't go to the doctor.[15] The reasons why so many of us avoid the doctor, the researchers note, is that we often find doctor's visits to be stressful and because we feel doctors don't give us adequate information on how to make the right lifestyle changes to improve our health. We also put off routine doctor's visits because we don't trust the American healthcare system—both for well-documented historical reasons[16] and because a majority of Black people in this country report enduring at least one negative experience with doctors—such as having to speak up to get proper care and feeling as if the pain they were experiencing was not taken seriously by their medical provider. Numerous studies in recent years have also revealed that far too often, Black patients are receiving inferior care compared to White patients for the same conditions.[17] Beyond this racial dynamic, men in general don't go to the doctor as often as women do,[18] and through informal conversations with friends and associates, I know it's something that many Black men don't prioritize. But as we age, one of the most important things we can do is

---

[15] University of Michigan - "Study: African American men say doctor visits are often a bad experience." July 26, 2011

[16] University of Michigan, "Understanding Black Distrust of Medicine," May 14, 2021

[17] American Bar Association: "Implicit Bias and Racial Disparities in Health Care." Vol. 43, No. 3: The State of Healthcare in the United States

[18] American Heart Association - "Misguided masculinity keeps many men from visiting the doctor." July 15, 2021

find a doctor we're comfortable with and build a relationship with them through routine checkups. Far too many of us are seeking medical care at the ER when our conditions are too far gone for medical intervention to make a difference. Black men are sicker than White men and too many of us are dying before our time of conditions that are treatable if they're caught early enough. We're less likely than our White peers to have our blood pressure under control and know our cholesterol levels. It doesn't have to be this way. Preventive care is the bedrock of our healthcare system today and it's the best way to stop the myriad chronic illnesses we're at high risk of developing in their tracks.

5. Therapy Is A Big Help

For those of us who've managed to get our foot in the door and establish careers in corporate America, the people in our lives may see us as Superman. I know I certainly saw my Uncle Juan that way and I suspect that my children and some of my loved ones may see me in a similar light. But as my diehard comic book heads can attest, even Superman has his kryptonite—moments of fatigue and weakness. Yet while Superman is blessed with a fortress of solitude, finding our place to recharge and restore our mental health isn't so simple. Noting the Superman analogy, Christopher Harvell, the entrepreneur, and former management consultant, says: "Sometimes because of that idealized perception, brothers don't feel comfortable taking off that cape, removing that S off their chest and saying, 'My feelings are hurt. I don't know if I can make this. I'm really, really sad right now. I have so much anxiety that I may be having trouble breathing. I'm having so much anxiety it's impacting my ability to get an erection. I'm having so much anxiety that I can't sleep." Therapy can be a place to let this all out. As noted earlier in this chapter, research shows that as we climb the socioeconomic ladder as Black men, we're at higher risk than anyone of developing anxiety and depression along the way. You can't just pray away anxiety and depression, or always unload your worries on others. In this regard, psychological counseling can be a valuable lifeline that can prevent the development or worsening of mental health issues. It's also a tool that can enhance your ability to cope with the inevitable stresses of corporate life.

6. Get Some Love In Your Life

Marriage may not be for everyone, but for men, the benefits of tying the knot are immense. In a major 2019 survey of 127,545 people, Harvard Health found that married men are healthier than men who never married or men whose marriages ended in divorce or widowhood. The research also found that married men live longer than men without spouses—with guys who marry after the age of twenty-five yielding the most benefits from wedlock. Why are married men healthier? Countless studies show that married people tend to eat better and are less likely to smoke and drink excessively.

Beyond boosting your health and longevity, research shows that marriage might also benefit your bank account in the long run. Numerous studies show that married men, especially those who work in corporate America, often earn more than their single counterparts. Finding the right partner matters, though. Being chained to a miserable relationship won't do your professional life or health any good.

7. Prioritize Time With Friends

My closest friends were the center of my world throughout my 20s. After grinding away at school or work, it'd be time to run the town and jump from party to party, or just get together for some good food, beer, and a little NBA2K.[19] Sometimes my best friend and I would laugh so hard during our hangouts that it'd feel like my stomach was about to burst. Little did I know back then how hard it would be to sustain all those relationships as the demands of corporate and family life came calling. Year by year, we'd gradually drift from seeing each other nearly every other day to catching up on weekends, and then maybe once a month through careful planning. By my 40s, weekends were filled with driving my kids to soccer games, recitals, and birthday parties, leaving little time for the laugh-filled hangouts with homies who used to nourish my soul. At best, I'd see all those close friends once or twice a year. Sure, we kept in daily contact through group chats and social media, but it wasn't the same.

Being a married family man is certainly a wonderful thing. But research shows that close relationships with your kids don't provide much of a benefit from a longevity standpoint. Quality friendships, on the other hand, can provide some dramatic benefits. A clinical review of nearly 150 studies found that people with stronger social relationships had a 50% greater likelihood of survival regardless of their age, gender, or health status.[20]

On the flip side, we're in the midst of a loneliness epidemic in our country, with scientists saying that loneliness is as damaging to our health as smoking.[21] Men are especially vulnerable

---

[19] NBA2k is a series of basketball simulation video games developed by Visual Concepts and published by 2K Sports. It's best known for its realistic gameplay. I was a hardcore player until my late 30s.
[20] National Library of Medicine – "Social Relationships and Mortality Risk: A Meta-analytic Review." July 2010
[21] The Guardian – "WHO declares loneliness a 'global public health concern." Nov. 21, 2023

to the dangers of loneliness because many of us struggle to express our feelings or forge genuine connections with others.

But it's important to remember that we've been designed by nature as social creatures and that true friends are a key component to living a healthy, well-rounded life. To maintain my relationships, I've begun to prioritize them just as I do other important aspects of life. My hangouts, which used to happen spontaneously, are now planned in advance and logged onto my Outlook and shared family calendar. Because as a corporate man, if it's not on the calendar, it ain't happening. And to survive The Weathering Effect, we need our friends.

CHAPTER TWO

AVOIDING THE ANGRY BLACK MAN STEREOTYPE

"To be a Negro in this country and to be relatively conscious is to be in a state of rage, almost, almost all the time—and in one's work."

—James Baldwin, 1961

"Justin—let me tell you something, man. And hear me clearly. You are large. You are loud. And you are Black. That shit's not gonna fly in the real world."

Dr. Mike Bush, my college journalism professor and faculty advisor, delivered these words of wisdom that I would never forget back in the fall of 2002 after I had gotten into a huge argument with the editor of our student newspaper. Dr. Bush is a large, deep-voiced Black man, whose presence is reminiscent of the professor Laurence Fishburne portrays in the 1995 film Higher Learning. His remarks were a reality check, and he delivered a valuable lesson about turning down the temperature in professional settings when disagreements arise.

I had begun my college career a bit later than normal. After graduating high school, I tried my hand at a series of failed entrepreneurial ventures and dead-end jobs before enrolling in a single English class at Long Island University, shortly before 9/11. Like many young people in their early twenties, I possessed a seriously underdeveloped level of self-awareness and I gave no thought to the fact that my height (I'm 6'3'), my deep voice, and my high-energy personality could be intimidating to others.

After finally enrolling full-time at LIU for the spring 2002 semester and taking on a full course load, I joined the school newspaper and quickly became a member of the editorial leadership team. By that point, I was a cocky 22-year-old who had just taken over as editor of the paper's Op-Ed section, and I was certainly a bit drunk with the power of the pen and control over a cool, new platform to reach thousands of students.

I had reduced the editor, a young Black woman, to tears with my tirade. To this day, I can't even remember the cause of that argument. It was probably some silly disagreement over an edit she wanted to make that I didn't like. But all these years later, I can't forget how shaken I'd left that young woman. That argument with the editor is one of the biggest regrets of my college career, which is why I remember it all these years later. It's a moment I deeply wish I could go back and do over. The relationship between that editor and I was irreparably damaged after that, and I'll forever live on in her mind as a total jerk. (If she even remembers that episode.)

The following summer, I landed an internship at Bloomberg News, where the diminutive Matt Winkler reigned supreme. He had famously built Bloomberg's news operation from a humble startup into a global, market-moving juggernaut—and he was well-known throughout the industry for both his trademark bowties and volcanic, red-faced tirades. That internship was my first taste of corporate life, and it wasn't lost on me that no Black man who expects to build a lasting and successful career could ever get away with the type of behavior that Winkler was known for.

During my two summers interning at Bloomberg, (I returned the following year,) I was fortunate enough to never directly witness a Matt Winkler tirade (or be the target of one,) but his temper was openly talked about in the newsroom by veteran staff reporters and editors. It was also a recurring topic in media outlets that covered the news industry in the early 2000s.

Legend has it that during a trip to Bloomberg's Tokyo bureau years ago, Winkler became so irate during a discussion at a restaurant meal with subordinates that he began yelling and forcefully banging a wall to emphasize his points. He allegedly banged the wall so hard that the lights at the venue began flickering, much to the consternation of diners at nearby tables.[22]

For any human being who works in a corporate setting, there will be times when you'll get angry—even justifiably so. At some point, most corporate lifers will feel the sting of getting passed over for a promotion or the frustration of not being given the credit they deserve. There are times when you may find your agenda stymied by bureaucracy or blocked by some other organizational hurdle. Frankly, you may even find yourself stuck, working with someone who you flat out just don't like. And if you're Black or a person of color, odds are you'll experience your share of microaggressions as well.

But for Black men in these settings, managing through anger is a tricky proposition, and loudly banging on walls in front of your colleagues, Winkler-style, isn't just a surefire way to hurt your brand within a company. It can even destroy your career. Anger is a normal emotion that we all experience. It's an emotional state that can vary in intensity from mild irritation to intense fury and rage.[23] It's

---

[22] Gawker, Jan. 4, 2008: "The Enemy is the Human!"
[23] Source: American Psychological Association: "Control anger before it controls you." Aug. 9, 2022

a natural, adaptive response to threats, and in a similar fashion to other emotions—it comes with physiological changes, such as an increase in heart rate, blood pressure, and skin temperature, along with a surge in the body's stress hormones, which include adrenaline and cortisol. When you're angry, the mind becomes sharpened and focused as your body's 'fight or flight' response to perceived danger kicks into gear. We've been hardwired by nature to respond to anger with aggression. For Black professional men operating in corporate environments, how you express anger, and who you express it in front of, matters. The Matt Winklers of the world are allowed to loudly and uncontrollably express anger in the workplace and still keep their jobs and lofty titles. Not so for others, especially Black men who are already walking a precarious social tightrope in predominantly White corporate spaces.

The comedian Dave Chappelle hilariously illustrates this fact in a 2004 episode of his sketch comedy program "Chappelle's Show." The sketch features a young Black executive named Vernon, who worked his way up from a family that's been stuck in the ghetto and mired in drug abuse for generations. Vernon is the classic rags-to-riches story, having studied diligently to become the class valedictorian in high school and later becoming the first person in his family to graduate from college. After graduation, Vernon grinds his way, all the way to the top, putting in 14-hour days, six days a week to become the youngest vice president in the history of the fictional ViaCorp Corporation. During a board meeting, his mentor—a White man—tries to praise Vernon's work by awkwardly asking Vernon in faux hip-hop dialect to "give him some skin."

Embarrassed by this microaggression, which made him feel like an Uncle Tom at a boardroom table filled with older White men, Vernon explodes with rage, dropping F-bombs, barking dog-like in a mimic of the late rapper DMX, and even shoving his mentor into a chair at one point. The sketch closes with Vernon, presumably fired from his cushy job with his career in tatters, now working as a gas station attendant.

The sketch succeeds because of how relatable it is. Most of us, at one point or another, have fantasized about telling off someone we don't like at work, or even quitting in a fit of rage while letting the boss know the real deal on the way out the door. But such scenes are meant to stay safely tucked within the realm of the imagination.

In reality, we are best served by maintaining a strong poker face and reserving moments for letting the frustration out in front of a trusted (and select) few. In fairness, this is an approach that anyone should take, regardless of race or gender, but there are special, historical reasons why Black men are forced to bear an even greater sense of self-awareness around this issue. We can trace the reason for this back to the days of America's antebellum past when the stereotype of the angry Black man first took shape.

What Is The Angry Black Man Stereotype?

The angry Black man stereotype originated during slavery when negative views about Black people were used to justify their inhumane treatment and exploitation. Back then, Black men were depicted as inherently violent, aggressive, hostile, and prone to anger. We were seen as beastly, subhuman, and in need of taming by a superior race. These views didn't disappear with Emancipation. Instead, over the past two centuries, they've evolved and become engrained within the fabric of the American psyche. Such views about Black men have been reinforced through media representations portraying us as hypermasculine criminals, gang members, and potentially dangerous people who have no business freely roaming the streets, let alone calling the shots in corporate America.

This is not just perception, research shows just how deeply embedded these views of Black men have become—and how dangerous they are. A 2017 study by the American Psychological Association found that people tend to perceive Black men as larger and more threatening than similarly sized white men.[24] The lead author of the study, John Paul Wilson, said the findings could help explain why Black men are more likely than their White peers to be shot by police. Additionally, a 2015 study from the University of California Los Angeles said people more often associate Black-sounding male names like DeShawn and Jamal, "with larger, more violent people," than they do with those who have "White-sounding names" like Connor or Garrett.[25]

These studies depict unconscious biases about Black males and illustrate how widespread they are. Whether we realize it or not, we all carry unconscious biases about our colleagues into work every day. I even came face-to-face with this type of bias during my time as a journalist at ABC News.

Oh Wow—You Look Like A Thug!

I'll never forget a microaggression that nearly pushed me over the edge during my days as a Production Associate for the ABC News Investigative Unit. Months after Bernard Madoff confessed to operating the largest Ponzi scheme in American history, I was sent to stake out his son Mark Madoff's apartment in New York's SoHo neighborhood. There was widespread belief in our newsroom that Mark and his brother Andrew had been in on their father's scheme, and so we were looking to capture them on camera, TMZ-style. The object of the assignment was to essentially ambush our target on camera and ask them, "What did you know about your father's scheme? Were you in on it?" As investigative journalists, our approach with this type of assignment was to remain as inconspicuous as possible,

---

[24] American Psychological Association, March 2017
[25] Vox, "A depressing study of how people respond to stereotypically black and white names," Oct. 9, 2015

and so for my Mark Madoff mission I threw on a dark hoodie and a Yankees cap.

When I got back to the newsroom, my boss, a White woman said to me with the brightest smile, "Oh wow—you look like a thug!" I knew from the look on her face and even from the vibe between us at the time that she didn't deliver those words with malicious or racist intent. I recall fake laughing at the remark at the time and then going about my business. But those words, which were delivered jokingly, dealt me a harsh reminder of who I could be seen as by my White colleagues with the simple swap of a business shirt and slacks for a hoodie and jeans: a thug. The phrase rang in my head for days after the incident, eventually curdling into a sense of disappointment and anger.

I didn't stay quiet about it either. After doing a slow boil for a few days, I went to my manager's superior—the network's senior investigative news correspondent—and casually told him about the remark. As far as I know, my manager wasn't disciplined for her insensitive words, but it felt good to get it off my chest and raise awareness of it anyway.

By February 2012, I was three years removed from my time at ABC News Investigative Unit when an incident in central Florida put into perspective just how dangerous my old manager's remark was. A Black 17-year-old boy who happened to be wearing a hoodie was walking through a gated community one evening after a quick trip to a convenience store to buy some Skittles and iced tea. He had been on the phone with his girlfriend at the time. Nevertheless, a neighborhood watchman—who was perhaps conditioned by the angry Black man stereotype—determined that the boy was suspicious. Thug-like, even. He called 911 to report the boy, and a short while later shot him dead, disregarding instructions from the operator not to approach him. Today, both Trayvon Martin and the hoodie he wore are Civil Rights icons that symbolize the potential dangers of being a Black male in our society.

Whether we are in a corporate setting or walking through a gated community, we are forced to take great pains to appear harmless and unthreatening, lest we trigger reminders of the angry Black man stereotype that still lingers within the American psyche.

Jerrell–You're Doing Great Work, But...

By all accounts, Jerrell was riding the type of professional high most people can only dream of. Jerrell, a Black, married father of twin 14-year-old boys, was excelling in his role as a senior program manager at a leading pharmaceutical firm. He had recently launched a new health equity initiative and earned rave reviews throughout the company for building the program from scratch while developing a sprawling cross-functional team to execute both its launch and long-term operation. At his mid-year review, Jerrell's manager made clear that for the most part, he was on a solid path to a senior management position with the firm. Even reaching the Managing Director level seemed like it was no longer just a pipe dream for Jerrell. There was just one catch.

"You've got to do a better job of handling your emotions when you're frustrated," his manager, who happens to be a Black woman, said. "You've got some people saying… 'I don't know about this dude. I've got to steer clear of him.' And then you've been venting about quitting when things aren't going your way. It's not a good look. Don't worry about any of this going in your official review, that's just the word on the street."

Those words, which came at the end of a review session that was filled with praise, rocked Jerrell with the force of a Mike Tyson jab to the jaw.

"In moments like that, your mind starts racing. You start replaying scenes from months past in your mind. You try to remember when you might've said or done something that led to this," he said. "That review put me into a deep funk for a few weeks because you start feeling as if you need to grow eyes in the back of your head, and that you can't freely go about doing your work and interacting with your colleagues."

Jerrell admits that at times he had been "less than friendly" on Zoom calls with colleagues from the firm's Marketing, Controls, and Legal departments while getting the health equity initiative up and running due to several "mind-numbing" bureaucratic issues that he says arose with each of those departments. After one of those calls, a colleague provided Jerrell with constructive feedback, noting that he had been a bit brusque with partners, although not overtly angry.

Jerrell adds that there were moments during the development of the project when the various departmental reviews seemed designed to prevent it from ever coming to market. He said he'd vented his frustrations to a couple of colleagues whom he thought would keep his angry rants and musings about moving onto another role or firm, private.

"Yes, there were times during this whole episode where I was just so taxed mentally and emotionally that I thought I couldn't do it anymore," Jerrell told me. "It's like pushing a boulder up a 100-foot hill all by yourself. And I made the mistake of opening up to people I thought I was speaking to in confidence. I was mortified when my manager said she knew I'd wondered aloud about quitting. I mean, who would want their manager to know something like that is on your mind? Or that you get emotional when you encounter a roadblock? This all felt like a death knell towards my career trajectory. Am I making Managing Director now? I've got to put that out of my mind for the time being."

Jerrell insists that while he may have on occasion flashed signs of frustration, and even anger, he's never openly demonstrated those feelings through yelling at others or being flat-out rude. "I'm passionate about my work, but I do care about my brand and how I'm perceived, so I've never tried to intimidate colleagues or try to be difficult," he says. "But hey, I'm human and I'm not good at masking my emotions, I guess."

Jerrell's experience raises questions about how Black men—and Black employees in general—are allowed to display and work through negative emotions such as anger, that inevitably arise in professional settings from time to time. In a 2010 paper, sociology professor Adia Harvey Wingfield published the results of a qualitative survey of twenty-five professional Black Americans (some of whom are women.)[26]

From those interviews, Wingfield concludes that many Black workers believe that rules governing the expression of feelings in the workplace are racialized in subtle ways that shackle them, even as they provide latitude for White workers to express the full range of emotions normally experienced at the office. Wingfield says, that depending on your profession, there are unspoken rules (also known as feeling rules) that dictate how you're allowed to express irritation and anger. For example, she says that attorneys have carte blanche to express anger at paralegals or secretaries. Cops, meanwhile, are free to do the same with suspects. And as we saw with Matt Winkler, a special set of so-called "feeling rules" for leadership in Bloomberg's newsroom enabled him to get away with decades of boorish behavior with impunity.

But for Black professional workers, different rules seem to apply. Wingfield says the twenty-five professionals she interviewed each held a belief that they were not permitted in their workplaces to show anger under any circumstances. In contrast, they "cite numerous examples of White workers who have openly expressed feelings of frustration or annoyance that are simply unavailable to them as Black employees."

Consider the example of Jay, a systems engineer who Wingfield interviewed for her survey. He told Wingfield:

> "One woman—management had a problem with her, with one of her presentations. The organization (of her

---

[26] "Are Some Emotions Marked "Whites Only?" Racialized Feeling Rules in Professional Workplaces," by Adia Harvey Wingfield, May 2, 2010.

presentation) wasn't tight, and she went off! 'What is it now? You guys are really getting on my nerves!' And I'm like, 'Wow, she's talking to her managers like that?' She's still there, nothing's wrong. They met with her, I heard her threaten to quit, and they were like, 'No—don't quit!' If it were me, they'd probably be like, 'All right!'... You know? So, they (whites) say what they want. If someone says, 'Do this,' they question it or get smart. If it were me, I'd be labeled as an angry Black dude, who can't get along with coworkers. But because it's them, it's all right."

Robert, a Black media executive, expressed similar sentiments to the BBC.[27] In an interview with the network, Robert said that if he gets too enthusiastic about a subject at work, the intent behind his emotions can be misinterpreted.

"I can see in their body language and their eyes that they're a bit scared of me when I'm going into full passion mode. I think as a Black man especially, that a lot of people are just scared of you anyway. You raise your voice slightly and you see the look. People don't say anything, but you see a look of fear."

Pressure Bursts Pipes: The Danger of Internalizing Anger

"Never let your emotions supersede your intelligence."

—Jadakiss

"Slowness to anger makes for deep understanding; a quick-tempered person stockpiles stupidity."

—Proverbs, 14:29

---

[27] BBC, "The People Penalized for Expressing Feelings at Work," Nov. 1, 2021

On the morning of my father's military funeral, just as I was about to set foot in the limousine that would take us to the Sarasota National Cemetery where he'd be buried alongside his fellow U.S. soldiers, the repo man showed up. It turns out that as cancer was ravaging his body during the previous five months, Dad decided to stop paying his car note. In a scene that could have been straight out of a great tragicomedy, I still chuckle a bit at the sight of my kid sister arguing with the repo man as he hooked my dad's red 2019 Nissan Altima up to his tow truck. (Spoiler alert: despite my sister's valiant effort, the repo man took the car as our limo drove away.)

Paul Grant did the best he could with what life gave him. At his core, he was a good man. When the time came for him to punch his ticket to eternity, there would be no life-changing monetary inheritance coming my way. But what I did inherit from the late, great Mr. Grant, however, was priceless: his effortless, unconscious, instinctive swagger.

My father was the essence of cool. He walked with a confident, smooth bop in his step—and despite lacking the funds for an expensive wardrobe, he possessed an innate sense of style that you just can't teach. He was comfortable talking to anyone and he had no problems making friends everywhere he went.

I, on the other hand, am the opposite of cool. I'm an absolute nerd to the core and much more comfortable at home, in libraries, and in bookstores than I am at parties, mingling with others. But I did manage to inherit my father's confident swagger, which played a crucial role in helping me to successfully navigate both the streets of pre-gentrified Brooklyn, as well as the offices of numerous Fortune 500 corporations.

As a Black male who came of age in Brooklyn in the 1990s—a land pockmarked by abandoned buildings, crack houses, stray dogs, and vicious battles between the Decepticons and Raiders gangs—I was compelled to learn and adopt the so-called "cool pose." Where I'm from, if you didn't carry yourself in a certain way, you'd have a hard time maneuvering around the neighborhood without the risk of being jumped, robbed—or worse.

The cool pose is a way of walking, talking, dressing, and mannerisms all contrived to help you define your masculinity as a Black man. We had our own versions of this in Clinton Hill, where I'm from—including a slang dialect that outsiders couldn't understand, which was by design. That pose was our armor against the world, where the statistics told you that many of us had already lost in the game of life even before we really had a chance to play. Some of our crew would go on to live productive lives, while others had their lives cut short through illness, violence, or massive prison sentences.

Beyond the mannerisms and style, the cool pose was about showing the world that we were unbothered. It was a mask we wore to demonstrate that we were always in control, no matter the circumstances. Showing any emotion was considered weak. Where I'm from, Black men learned early on to internalize anger and hurt feelings, much to our mental—and physical detriment.

Coincidentally, just as the cool pose served as a shield where I grew up, it continues to serve as a shield in corporate spaces where we're in the minority. Although the mannerisms, style, and comportment I use now are markedly different than the ones I was forced to deploy during my adolescence, that mask of confidence and maintenance of a cool exterior in the face of unrelenting social pressures remains the same.

One layer beneath the surface of that cool exterior, of course, is fear. A deep-rooted fear that with one misstep, I could lose everything I've worked so hard for and be transported back to where I came from in an instant—much like Chappelle's Vernon character, who finds himself back in poverty after losing his cool in the worst possible way in one unfortunate moment of temporary insanity.

If you peel back another layer, you'll find exhaustion. Deep, existential exhaustion from the grind of putting on the cool pose, day after day, from adolescence through adulthood. I've found that the pressure I've personally felt to internalize negative emotions is virtually universal among Black men, and it's a challenge that's persisted for generations.

The late activist and tennis champion Arthur Ashe—the only Black man to win singles titles at Wimbledon, the U.S. Open, and the Australian Open— spoke out about this challenge in the 1980s. He had been forced to adopt a different version of the cool pose as an adolescent who came of age in Virginia in the 1950s at the height of the Civil Rights Movement. Ashe's cool pose was far different than the one we adopted in 1990s Brooklyn. Ashe's pose was anchored in remaining stoic and poised in the face of racism in the Jim Crow-era South.

Ashe was coached and mentored by Dr. Robert Johnson, the putative godfather of Black tennis. Johnson famously converted his backyard into a tennis court, where he taught hundreds of Black children the sport—including the legendary women's champion Althea Gibson. Dr. Johnson was careful about the prospects that he decided to invest his time and energy in. Knowing the indignities that his Black players would face in a virtually all-White sport in the South, Gibson would only choose prospects based on their ability to remain calm, cool, and collected in hostile, unwelcome environments. Arthur Ashe fit the bill. Ashe calmly recollects the racial slurs, mean-spirited remarks, and gawking he often endured as the only Black child at tennis tournaments throughout the 1950s.

But by the time he turned 36—just four years after making history at Wimbledon—Ashe suffered a heart attack while hosting a tennis clinic, and he endured two bypass surgeries over four years. Although Ashe attributed his heart troubles to a congenital issue and heredity (his father suffered two heart attacks,) he said he "firmly" believed that bottling up emotions contributed to his cardiovascular problems.[28]

---

[28] Citizen Ashe, 2021

Medical research supports Ashe's suspicion that years of pent-up anger and frustration were putting his health at risk. For example, a 2009 study by the Stress Research Institute of Stockholm University found that men who bottled up anger after being treated unfairly at work are up to five times more likely to suffer a heart attack than those who allowed their frustrations to show.[29]

In a study of 2,755 employed men over eleven years, the researchers found that those who resorted to letting points of frustration with colleagues or management pass without saying anything were up to two to five times more likely to develop heart disease than those who were more confrontational at the office.

In addition to the threat unaired frustrations pose to cardiovascular health, repressed anger comes with significant mental health risks as well. According to Psychology Today internalized anger that's not given a healthy valve for release can eventually lead to depression, paranoia, and passive-aggressive behavior—all of which are issues that will negatively impact personal relationships, as well as one's overall quality of life. (Each of these issues will prevent you from operating at the peak performance you'll need to consistently win in corporate America.) Relationships are the lifeblood for building a lasting and successful career, and paranoia and passive-aggressive behavior are a surefire way to sabotage your brand over the long term.)

In a 1986 guest column for *The New York Times*, Ashe wrote that he witnessed physical and emotional difficulties among his Black male friends who went on to careers in the corporate world. Like Ashe, each of these men had been socialized to internalize anger and frustration. Although this group of friends certainly enjoyed the material benefits of career paths that had been essentially closed off before the Civil Rights Movement, the fruits of their labor came at a high physical and psychological cost.

---

[29] Reuters, "Speak up: a study shows stifling anger at work can kill. Nov. 23, 2009

My 39-to 45-year-old Black professional buddies have paid a very heavy emotional toll," Ashe wrote in *The New York Times*. "Divorce is the norm rather than the exception. Nearly everyone is hypertense. The stress is barely bearable most of the time, but it is hidden behind ingenious subterfuges. I am not the only one to have had a heart attack before age 40—and I was in excellent physical condition. Most of my friends are frustrated, and some are now visiting shrinks—something our older Black professionals rarely did. Black shrinks themselves are grossly overscheduled.

In a similar fashion to the subjects Wingfield interviewed for her survey, Ashe openly expressed frustration at feeling forced to bottle up his emotions on the tennis court, while White male contemporaries like Jimmy Connors and John McEnroe were free to behave as boorishly as they wished. Speaking of McEnroe, who was well-known for his on-court tantrums, Ashe had this to say:

> "McEnroe had the emotional freedom to be a bad boy. I never had that emotional freedom. If I had been like that, I am convinced the tennis world would have driven me out of it. My race wouldn't allow me to be like that … And so, when I see John going off half-cocked, I'm very irritated at him and I am envious because I would like to do the same thing. But I don't feel I have that luxury."

Conclusion: 5 Tips for Black Men on Processing Anger in Corporate Spaces

"I'm mad as hell and I'm not going to take this anymore!"

—Howard Beale,
a fictional character from the 1976 film, Network.

1. **Internalized anger is hazardous to your health. Deep-breathing exercises are an effective release valve.**

   As Black men, we've been socialized to adopt some version of the cool pose to avoid giving off the appearance of negative emotions, like anger. In many of our communities, expressing the full range of our emotions has been stigmatized, and letting your guard down or showing frustration, anger, and even sadness is widely seen as a form of weakness. For well-documented historical and sociological reasons, it's a painful reality that Black men who work in corporate spaces simply don't enjoy the same freedoms as their White colleagues to express their frustrations in professional settings. (We've got the nasty old specter of the angry Black man stereotype to contend with.) As a result, it's natural that many of us may feel compelled to internalize anger.

   But while completely losing your temper and flying off the handle like Chappelle's Vernon character is entirely out of the question, it's important to find safe mechanisms for releasing work-related anger. Repressed anger poses significant mental and physical health risks over the long term, so holding it in simply isn't sustainable. Over the years, deep breathing has become one of my go-to methods for calming myself down when I feel my temper starting to flare up. I'm a big fan of the simple triangle breathing exercise, which involves inhaling deeply for three seconds, holding that breath for another three, and then exhaling for three seconds. I repeat this exercise for a few minutes. Another good one is the so-called 4-7-8 breathing technique. You begin by breathing in through your nose for four seconds. Next, you hold your breath for seven seconds. And then you exhale forcefully for eight. The cycle is most effective when you repeat it up to four times.[30]

Deep-breathing exercises like this one can shut off the 'fight or flight' instinct that kicks in when you're angry, and it can ease and even reverse the physiological changes to your body that come with anger, which include an increase in heart rate and blood pressure.

2. It's Okay To Vent Every Once In A While. But As A Go-To Mechanism, It's Limited—And Can Even Be Destructive.

We've all done this at some point. You find that sympathetic ear to turn to at work or home and you bitch. You let off some steam. Whether it's about some mind-numbing new process that's been added to your role, an annoying colleague, or a micromanaging boss who's making your days miserable, there's a good chance that if you work in corporate America, you've felt the need to vent at some point. And to be frank, a little venting now and then is healthy, particularly when you're doing it with another co-worker. Occupational psychologists say this type of exchange can help bring colleagues closer together and make it easier to cope in difficult professional settings. And certainly, talking to a loved one, friend or trusted colleague about issues that are making you angry at work can help you deepen those relationships. But beware of doing this too often, because it can wind up fueling the negative effects

---

[30] Medical News Today, Jan. 11, 2023

of your anger. It also does nothing to address or solve the root causes of whatever it is that's causing your anger.

"Prolonged or repeated venting can become counterproductive," says Firdaus S. Dhabhar, Ph.D., a professor at the University of Miami Miller School of Medicine's Department of Psychiatry, Department of Microbiology and Immunology, and Sylvester Comprehensive Cancer Center.[31] "When your venting becomes chronic and you keep venting to one person after another, it can increase, rather than decrease your chronic stress."

If you decide to vent to someone at work, it's important to exercise extreme caution. Be sure that whomever you talk to has genuine care and capacity to hear you and provide constructive feedback. If not, you run the risk of becoming a topic of office gossip. And even if you find a truly sympathetic ear with a colleague, be sure not to overburden them with your problems. They've got their own challenges to deal with.

3. **Change Your Environment**

I can think of few things more upsetting in modern life than sitting through an unpleasant meeting. A meeting where your work is being questioned by a superior or having a tense conversation with a coworker who is difficult to collaborate with is quite jarring. One of my go-to strategies for calming down after a difficult situation at work is to get up, head for the door, and go for a stroll. I'm a big proponent of taking leisurely walks during the workday if your schedule allows it, and this is an especially important tool for easing the tension in your body if something's caused you to become angry at the office. I've spent a good chunk of my career working in gorgeous waterfront locations, which is a plus for scenic

---

[31] UHealth Collective, "Venting: Is it Helpful or Harmful?" March 21, 2022

walks. But the key here is to give yourself a break. A short break and breath of fresh air can help you refocus. Also, a little physical movement can go a long way toward reducing the stress that's fueling your anger. (And if the weather isn't cooperating, take a stroll to the breakroom for some water, or the company café if your company has one. Maybe there's even a Starbucks nearby.) Wherever you go, a brief change of the environment is a big help when your anger is flaring.

4. Channel Your Anger Into Meaningful Action

Sometimes, a little anger can be a good thing, and it can even catalyze meaningful, positive change. I've experienced moments in my career where I've been angry about being stuck in roles that have seemingly offered no path to meaningful growth in responsibility or pay. There've been times I've been angry about being tethered to an awful boss and I've been angry about feeling marginalized and underestimated as well. In those moments, I've channeled that anger towards helping me identify and focus on the things I really want. Periods like this have motivated me to dig deep and reach for more. It's driven me to network for new opportunities both internally and externally. And on multiple occasions, it's led to both significant increases in pay and promotions.

A good friend of mine who led marketing for a major media company was once angry about the dysfunctional environment he was forced to work in due to a toxic boss. That anger motivated him to get an MBA. For two years he took classes at night while he endured a difficult work situation. After completing his degree, he quit that job and launched his marketing agency. Five years later, his agency has employed more than fifteen people and has enjoyed successive years of revenues north of $5 million. (He even took on his old firm as a client and made a nice chunk of money off them!)

In his case, that anger didn't drive him to rant and rave like a lunatic. Instead, it motivated him to get strategic and it wound up changing his life for the better.

5. If The Situation Calls For It—Speak Up For Yourself (With Tact)

As a racial minority in a predominantly White professional setting, speaking up for yourself can feel a little daunting. But when you're faced with a situation that's causing you justifiable anger—such as a microaggression or a toxic work situation that can be corrected, remaining silent simply isn't an option. You can even harness anger strategically to help you gain status.

For example, I was once angry about being overworked while at a company that had ample resources to invest in adding headcount to support me. I didn't stay quiet about it. Instead, I drew up a new organizational structure and created a plan to fund the role. Almost immediately my managers signed onto my plan, and I gained not one—but two people to support my work. That new status put me on track for a promotion and a dramatic bump in pay that came in less than two years.

Research also shows that anger, as opposed to mere emotional expression, can be leveraged as a tool for gaining power and control. A 2001 study in *The Journal of Personality and Psychology* found that people grant more status to colleagues and politicians who express anger rather than sadness or guilt.[32]

Above all, recognize that if you stay silent, you're doing your body, mind, career, and those who depend on you a disservice if you just sit there and take whatever is causing your anger.

---

[32] American Psychological Association, "When anger's a plus," March 2003, Vol 34, No. 3

CHAPTER THREE

BUILDING A ROADMAP FOR YOUR CAREER

"We forge the chains we wear in life."

—Charles Dickens

May 18, 2018, is a date I remember clearly for two reasons. The first is that it was a moment of triumph because it was the day my wife, Anika, received her Executive MBA from Rutgers Business School. The second reason I remember that day so clearly is because her graduation provided me with a much-needed day off from my personal hell: my new job as a VP at Goldman Sachs.

Being stuck in a job you hate with every fiber of your being is hell. Being stuck in a *new job* that you realize you hate is a *special* kind of hell because there's no easy way out of that type of jam. In my case, the idea of crawling back to my previous employer was a non-starter. They'd made me a counteroffer, which I rejected since it didn't measure up to the Goldman package in terms of dollars, seniority, or even a path to a leadership role. Beyond that, the company—a mid-sized fund management firm—was a big, fat takeover target, and I had no interest in riding out the rollercoaster of them being acquired, particularly since they didn't see me as senior management material.

As my family and I celebrated my wife and her classmates at the gorgeous New Jersey Performing Arts Center in Newark on that beautiful May afternoon, I was haunted by a sobering thought. It wasn't Goldman Sachs' fault that I was so miserable in my new role. Despite the loftier title and bigger paycheck, I reached rock bottom professionally, and the blame for my being there was entirely on me. May 18, 2018, was the day I accepted a painful truth. I had taken that Goldman job for all the wrong reasons: money, ego, and the lure of a more senior title at the most storied bank on Wall Street. I learned the hard way that if these are your core motivations—you'll never truly be happy in your career.

From the moment the recruiter reached out to me on LinkedIn, I was blinded by the Goldman mystique. Throughout multiple rounds of interviews, as well as a ridiculously challenging test to land the job, I never stopped to consider how the role aligned with my skills, values, or what I sought to get out of my career. I didn't stop to do the necessary homework to truly understand whether it was a fit for me.

The only thing that motivated me back then was a desire to get MINE—especially after one of my professional rivals got promoted to VP at my prior employer, while I didn't. Although this rival and I started at the same level, it didn't take long before it was clear that he was on a fast track to a senior leadership role while I wasn't.

Now, don't get me wrong. My rival happened to be a talented young White dude who deserved his success. But he had an influential executive sponsor doing the necessary blocking and tackling to help him forge a path to the next level. Despite glittering reviews and a superstar reputation of my own, I didn't have an influential leader in my corner sponsoring me for a promotion.

So, I found myself stuck, which left me jealous, angry, and nursing a New York-sized chip on my shoulder. My jealousy and frustration drove me towards that Goldman job and blinded me to the most fundamental questions you must ask yourself before taking a new role, including:

1. Is this how I want to spend my time?
2. Is this the life I want to live?
3. How does this new job fit into the story I want to tell about who I am and what I do?
4. How does this job align with the overarching vision that I have for my life and career?"

Announcing my resignation and sharing with colleagues I was headed to Goldman filled me with pride. I walked the halls of my soon-to-be former employer with a little extra swagger in my step because I'd reached the next level at a much more prestigious firm. They may not have seen me as a VP at that moment—but the biggest, baddest bank on Wall Street certainly did.

I figured that with a few years under my belt at Goldman, I'd be able to write my own ticket and eventually trade up on that position for another cushy, high-paying gig. Getting that stamp as a Goldman alumnus does carry some value. But by my third week into that job, I knew that I'd made a massive mistake in taking it. On the morning after her graduation, I said to my wife: "I can't even understand why this job exists."

It's About Your Legacy—Not Your LinkedIn Profile

"People rarely succeed unless they have fun in what they are doing."

—Dale Carnegie

The day I announced my new Goldman position on LinkedIn was my sole career highlight of 2018, the most difficult year of my professional life. One by one the comments came: "Way to future-proof your life, man! You're a superstar, Justin! You're going to CRUSH Goldman, dude." Those words of encouragement were intoxicating. And fleeting. After a couple of days of cheap dopamine hits from all those likes and comments on my job update, it was time to get on with my sad new reality. DAY AFTER DULL ASS DAY, I trudged into work, while doing my best to squeeze a few positives out of some difficult, self-inflicted circumstances.

Coincidentally, during the darkest period of my career, I enjoyed a front-row seat to my wife's ascent to her professional peak. From the depths of my misery, I drew inspiration from the fact that Anika's career rock-bottom moment—which hadn't been too long ago was the catalyst for her decision to go on a journey of self-reflection where she finally discovered what she wanted to do with the rest of her professional life. If she could find her way—maybe I could do the same, I figured.

Anika's journey began during the tumultuous summer of 2016. For the prior four years, she'd been part of the Essence Communications leadership team that produced their signature live events, including the Essence Festival—(which is the unofficial annual family reunion for Black America over the Fourth of July holiday in New Orleans.) Anika played a leading role for Essence in helping large brands like McDonald's, Wal-Mart, State Farm, Coca-Cola, and others deepen their connection to Black consumers through cool, live experiences.

But by August of that year, Anika had reached a breaking point. She'd been repeatedly stymied in her attempts to climb the ranks at Essence. After four years of doing stellar work in a volatile corporate environment marked by frequent mass layoffs, multiple sales to new owners, and two moves to new corporate headquarters—she'd had enough. On a brilliantly sunny August day, as we sat by the gorgeous Hudson River waterfront at Brookfield Place in Manhattan, Anika dropped a bomb on me.

"I've decided to enroll at the Rutgers Business School, and I'm going to take out a loan to pay for it," she said as we lunched on delicious ham-and-cheese sandwiches from the renowned French market, Le District. "I'll be done with the program in 14 months, but it's a move I've got to make now. And the classes begin in two weeks."

With no hesitation, I told her to go for it—cost and childcare logistics for our two young children[33] be damned. As we ate lunch, Anika sketched out a rough outline for her new career plan. The first step was to take a leap and enroll in Rutgers' MBA program for corporate executives. She was blocked from professional development opportunities at Essence due to her job level and decided that an Executive MBA would be her best path to the information she'd need to expand her knowledge base, skill set, and professional network. The second step was to learn all the ins and outs of operating a business, and so she selected entrepreneurship as a focus for her studies. Step three was to launch her own business.

Anika had grown tired of tap dancing to get a seat at the grown-up's table at Essence. Instead, she'd decided to build her own.

"I remember seeing all these amazing stories at that time of Black women who were running successful businesses that they'd built from nothing, and I remember thinking to myself: 'If they can start something, why can't I'," Anika said. "And as I leaned into this journey, I realized that I come from a rich lineage of entrepreneurs—including my grandfather, who ran his own pharmacy on the South Side of Chicago, and my grandmother, who launched and operated a nursery school."

After reflecting on the jobs that she'd had the most fun in during her career, Anika was certain that entrepreneurship was her path. She'd most enjoyed roles where she'd been given a blank slate to build an organization or new program from the ground up.

---

[33] At the time we had two children, a son, and a daughter. In 2021 we added a third child—our second daughter—to our brood.

"It clicked for me during my time at Rutgers," she said. "I recognized that I'd be at my happiest professionally in a setting where I had the freedom to develop a company from scratch. I didn't enjoy places where I was told, 'Well, we do things in this particular way because we've always done it that way.' Starting my own (experiential marketing) business was the clearest path towards working how I want to work."

In building out her new career roadmap, Anika found answers to two critical questions that are at the core of every successful, fulfilling career:

1. What motivates you?
2. Why are you on your current path?

When you don't know the answers to these questions, you run the risk of winding up like me at Goldman—where you're in a job that's a bad fit both for you and the company.

Career motivators are those elements that get your juices flowing and energize you for work every day. They help you maintain your resolve through all the bullshit that comes with work—whether you're working in some corporation or running your own business. Through my two decades of experience in corporate America (which includes plenty of trial-and-error along the way,) I've found there are generally three core motivators for us all. These include:

1. **Your contribution:** What you contribute to the world every day through your talents and those skills you've spent so many years developing. We're most fulfilled by our work when we're contributing to the world in areas that we're most passionate about in ways that we're good at.

2. **Your lifestyle:** This involves everything from your salary and where you live, to the hours you work and the flexibility you need in your schedule to support the areas of your life that matter the most to you.

3. **Your work environment:** This includes those elements in your workplace that are most important to you—such as the corporate culture, the physical environment of your workspace, and even the role you play in the organization.

We're at our happiest when we're in roles in which all three of our career motivators are being served. (You'll find that your career motivators may evolve across the different stages of your professional journey.) My career veered off track because I was applying my skills within the wrong professional context in a way that didn't satisfy my career motivators.

Although the Goldman job certainly paid enough to support the lifestyle I wanted to provide for my family, it was a serious mismatch in terms of the contribution it enabled me to make to the world. It was also a work environment mismatch for me.

During that long year of reflection in 2018, I reached the conclusion that I'd be at my happiest in a job that enabled me to tap into some of my extrovert tendencies. No matter how well a job paid me or how prestigious the company might be, I couldn't be tethered to a desk all day, alone, as I was at Goldman. I needed to be in a role that enabled me to get out of the office and work directly with clients and communities. I also wanted the freedom to be strategic and 'intrapreneurial[34].' My Goldman job was much more operational and tactical than I'd bargained for and wasn't the type of environment or culture that provided room for the spontaneous collaboration or creativity that I crave.

Chase Purpose And Happiness In Your Work

Working hard for something we don't care about is called stress. Working hard for something we love is called passion.

—Simon Sinek, author

---

[34] Intrapreneurship is a manner of work that enables an employee to operate like an entrepreneur within an organization. Employees who enjoy this style of work are self-motivated and proactive about how to innovate new ways of driving business.

By 2022, as the world continued its long slog out of the depths of the COVID-19 pandemic, corporate professionals everywhere reached their limits. Job unhappiness surged to an all-time high,[35] with 60% of employees taking the drastic step of "quiet quitting" their jobs.[36]

And while the pandemic ushered in an unprecedented new era of job flexibility, with remote and hybrid work becoming the new normal across industries, workers cited a long list of reasons for their unhappiness—including unfair treatment, corporate policies, favoritism, and mistreatment by colleagues.[37]

Meanwhile, the social justice movement that took off during the pandemic ignited "The Great Reflection,[38]" in which growing numbers of employees began to look inward and reexamine how they spend their time, energy, and social capital. Following this period of self-reflection, the research firm Gartner found that corporate professionals are increasingly craving purpose in their work. This is a big reason why employment in the non-profit space is now growing three times as fast as it is in the private sector.[39]

This epidemic of job unhappiness has taken a big toll on companies and has cost the global economy some $7.8 trillion in lost productivity.[40] But the human toll of this unhappiness is even more significant when you consider that each day you spend in a corporate job you dislike is a day of your life that you won't get back.

I've certainly endured my share of loathsome corporate jobs that were just a means to an end. It's often a necessary evil if only to make ends meet. If this happens to be you, just make sure it's temporary and

---

[35] CNBC – "Job unhappiness is at a staggering all-time high, according to Gallup." Aug 12, 2022.
[36] HRD Connect – "Quiet quitting - the silent threat to modern workplaces." June 12, 2024
[37] Gallup – "State of the Global Workplace." 2024 report
[38] Gartner – "Employees Seek Personal Value and Purpose at Work. Be Prepared to Deliver." March 29, 2023
[39] Washington Post - "The real reason America's nonprofit sector is seeing massive growth, and more!" May 12, 2023
[40]

that you have an exit plan. If you sit in a job for too long without tapping into your passions or taking tangible steps towards turning your dreams into a reality, you run the risk of living out the pain of Langton Hughes' famous poem, "A Dream Deferred." The poem, which Hughes published in 1951, painfully articulates the experience of watching dreams and ambitions that aren't nurtured wither and die.[41]

You Control Your Destiny - Not Hiring Managers Or Recruiters

"It's choice—not chance, which determines your destiny"

—Jean Nidetch
Founder, Weight Watchers

Despite my utter loathing of my Goldman job, I didn't immediately race for the exits. Instead, I operated on autopilot for a year and spent that time reflecting on what I truly wanted to do with my life and career.

(To make the best of it, I took advantage of some of the sweet perks that come from being a Goldman employee, which include an on-site gym and steam room. I went to both every day and got into the best shape of my life! That made the tedium somewhat bearable.)

Building a career roadmap means doing the hard work of creating a route from where you are to where you want to be. From the moment I graduated from college and entered the job market, I forfeited that responsibility and instead allowed recruiters and hiring managers to steer the direction of my career without ever giving real thought to the steps I'd need to take to actualize my dreams. I had also gotten so

---

[41] "A Dream Deferred" is part of Langston Hughes' broader work, "Montage of a Dream Deferred," a book-length poem published in 1951. He wrote the poem against the backdrop of the post-World War II economic boom, of which Black Americans were systematically shut out from participating in the various mechanisms that allowed their White peers to build generational wealth.

wrapped up in the day-to-day drudgery of corporate life that I'd even forgotten my dreams. That's the definition of a true sellout.

In doing so, I'd set myself on a path towards end-of-life regrets and the tragic statement that I've heard one too many older people make: "I wish I would have…" or "If only I would have…."

In building my career roadmap, I kept reliving my final conversation with my grandfather, Herbert Simpson. Over breakfast at his 13th floor apartment in Brooklyn's Atlantic Terminal on a bitterly cold morning in late January 2005, he told me something that I will carry to my grave: "You DON'T' get the TIME back." He said it with a wistful, haunted tint in his eyes. I don't remember everything we discussed on that fateful morning, but those words were forever imprinted on my consciousness. He reminded me that finality hangs over us all and that our days are numbered, even if we don't realize it. We've got to make each day count. (Two weeks after that breakfast, my grandfather departed this world at the age of 91.)

Towards the end of 2018, as the Goldman chapter in my life story drew to a close, I achieved the one thing in my career that I'd lacked to that point: a clear sense of what I wanted to do. I knew that I would no longer work in jobs that provided zero connection to what I wanted my life's work to be, no matter how prestigious the firm or how senior the title they were offering. My career would now be about more than making money and hustling on a hamster wheel of mindless, meaningless consumption between pay cycles. I felt a call towards service and the next step in my journey would be anchored on community impact. I didn't know exactly where that call would lead just yet, but I had a newfound sense of direction on where I was headed.

Around that time, Anika was in the final months of her seven-year run at Essence. She'd given them a date for her departure from the company and began building her new business, Idlewild Experiential. In addition to seizing the control she craved to develop a business in her own image, Anika's company would be anchored on community impact as well. Idlewild Experiential's foundational principle is to help corporations connect to diverse audiences through unforgettable live events and innovative campaigns. Anika set out to change how corporations engage with people of all backgrounds. But her resolve would soon be tested.

Build Your Roadmap—And Then Be Faithful Enough To STAY On It

"Hold the vision. Drop the excuses. Remember your why. Swerve around obstacles. Trust the process. Happiness and success will find you."

—Karen Salmansohn, author

I wish I could tell you that getting to the dream destination on your career roadmap is as simple as going from point A, to point B and then C. It never is. Even after you commit to a roadmap, there will be all sorts of obstacles and shiny temptations that will send you on a detour if you're not careful. You've got to fight to keep your dreams alive because there will always be a circumstance tempting you to do the practical thing and say forget it. Most people take the easy way out, and as time goes by, their dreams wither and die on the vine like autumn leaves.

The challenge of keeping your dreams alive brings to mind a scene from the 2009 film *Up in the Air,* in which the actor George Clooney stars as Ryan Bingham—a corporate consultant whose job is to fly across the country during the Global Financial Crisis and fire people on behalf of large corporations. In a memorable scene, he fires Bob, a middle-aged father who is now fearful of the future because of his newly unemployed status. Bob becomes visibly distressed and overwhelmed with anger and desperation after learning he's been laid off, worrying aloud about paying for his daughter's education and all the financial obligations that come from being your family's breadwinner.

Ryan, in a rare show of humanity after giving someone the axe, breaks from the usual HR script for layoffs and reminds Bob of a fateful decision he'd made after graduating from college. Bob dreamed of becoming a chef and bussed tables at a high-end restaurant when he was still in school. But instead of pursuing that dream after graduation, Bob took a corporate job that he didn't really want in exchange for a decent paycheck.[42] During the layoff, Ryan fills Bob with hope by convincing him to pursue the career he once dreamed of now that he's unshackled from a job that sent him on a detour.

Anika could certainly relate to Bob's thought process—pursue the dream or take the pragmatic route? In December of 2018, just as she was departing Essence and moving into her self-created role as CEO of Idlewild Experiential, multiple companies offered to pay her to give up on her dream of building and then running her own company. The first temptation came from an industry peer who'd launched a similar agency a year prior. This particular company was quickly gaining momentum, and she approached Anika about joining as a salaried employee.

The compensation package she'd dangled in front of Anika was a substantial raise above her Essence salary, and it even included a minority ownership stake. It was enough to make Anika stop and think about it. With two young children and a mortgage hanging over our head, plus those stubborn New Jersey property taxes and student loan payments for that MBA, it certainly seemed appealing to go to an established company. But Anika stayed firm.

"I just knew there was more that I could do. I had to stay faithful to the plan I'd set for myself," Anika said. "Deep down I knew— why should I build a company for someone else when I could do this on my own? I would have always regretted not sticking to my plan to build Idlewild."

---

[42] In fairness to Bob, millions of Americans make the same practical decision because they are saddled with overwhelming student loan debt.

The temptations and obstacles didn't stop there. Like a toddler stumbling around while learning how to walk, Idlewild endured some early misadventures out of the gate. Like every new business, there were kinks to iron out. After one of Idlewild's early corporate projects completely flopped, Anika once again got an opportunity to veer off her roadmap and take the easy way out when Digital Undivided—a nonprofit that helps Black women and Latina entrepreneurs grow their businesses—approached her about a senior-level job opportunity.

For a second time in a matter of months, Anika had an enticing role in front of her that offered the potential to earn dramatically more than what she'd been bringing in. The role was so tempting that Anika made it towards the later rounds of the process and anticipated that an offer was forthcoming.

"I did a lot of soul-searching in that moment and asked myself, 'What's it going to be?'" she said. "Ultimately, I pulled out of the running because it was a job that focused on providing funding to women entrepreneurs of color. I knew if I took that job, I would always wish that I could be on the other side as one of the businesses that Digital Undivided provided funding to. I just couldn't give up on Idlewild."

> *"Work to become—not to acquire."*
>
> —Eldert Hubbard,
> writer, artist, philosopher

Within 90 days of committing to a new direction for my professional life, doors that I couldn't imagine even existed began to open.

The first was a high-profile new initiative called Advancing Black Pathways, which JPMorgan Chase created to strengthen the economic foundation of Black communities around the world. The work involved harnessing the resources of the world's largest bank[43]

---

[43] JPMorgan Chase is the world's largest bank in terms of market capitalization as of March 21, 2024.

to create programs and targeted investments aimed at growing Black wealth through investing and entrepreneurship, career opportunities from entry level up to the boardroom, and delivering educational resources for students at Historically Black Colleges and Universities. The program was unlike anything I'd ever seen throughout my years in the financial services industry, and JPMorgan Chase was looking for someone to lead global communications for it. It was exactly the type of work I was searching for, and my heart skipped a beat when I first read the job description. Although I'd never officially been the head of communications for any firm, I thought it aligned with my background and skill set. So, I threw my name in the mix for the job, said a few prayers, and was thrilled to land the role a few weeks after applying and going through multiple rounds of interviews. The morning after I accepted the position, I handed in my resignation letter to Goldman Sachs.

"Where'd we go wrong," my Goldman manager asked me, stunned by my departure, especially since it came less than a week after we received our bonus checks. "This has nothing to do with you, the team, or the firm," I told him. "This is entirely on me. I just have to accept that this role simply isn't me—it's not the type of work I want to do. I'd honestly be doing both you and this company a major disservice by staying here any longer."

The second opportunity that fell in my lap was a professorship at my alma mater, Long Island University. Just two weeks before the Spring 2019 semester was to begin, the head of the university's journalism department, Dr. Donald Bird, called me with some urgent news. The professor they'd lined up to teach two journalism classes was no longer able to do it and I was the first person that came to mind as a replacement. I'd never taught before in a classroom setting, but always dreamed of becoming a college professor. So, I accepted the position immediately, and throughout a mid-winter weekend, developed the syllabi for both courses and immediately dove into a semester's worth of work.

In a similar fashion to Anika, I endured some early stumbles out of the gate with both positions since they were jobs I'd never done before. Starting a new role is intense enough and doing it while serving as a first-time adjunct professor with a two-class course load was far from easy. Preparing lectures and lesson plans is harder than it looks! But after a couple of weeks of doing both jobs, I found my footing. What resulted was one of the most rewarding chapters of my career. Because I was intellectually engaged and energized, I continually brought fresh, innovative ideas to both. With my rock-bottom moment becoming a distant memory, I poured in some of the best work of my professional life which led to even better opportunities down the line.

Within two years, I was promoted to Executive Director at JPMorgan Chase. And appointed to the Board of Trustees at Long Island University, where I've since led numerous initiatives to provide more than $100,000 scholarships to students in need—including a scholarship that I created in the name of my late Uncle, Juan Simpson.

Meanwhile, Anika has developed Idlewild Experiential into a multimillion-dollar business with a handful of full-time employees. She's succeeded in flipping all the knowledge she gained at Essence and Rutgers into a thriving company that's served many large corporate clients, including Amazon, Netflix, Disney, Gilead Sciences, SoFi, and more.

Neither Anika nor I see the jobs we're in now as the final destination for our careers. A career is a long, winding journey with countless twists, turns, ups, and downs. But we've both established roadmaps. My roadmap—no matter what firm I may happen to work for—points me towards opportunities that will enable me to drive positive impact for communities at scale. Today I am doing that work within the confines of one of the largest, most influential banks and as a trustee at a large university. Tomorrow, I may be serving communities within an entirely different professional context.

It's a journey I've remained faithful to, even when shiny temptations come along, beckoning me to veer off plan. Over the past few years, I've turned down multiple positions, including a chief of staff role for the CEO of a major financial services firm, as well as a chance to lead communications for another chief executive. Both opportunities would have prevented me from developing the areas of my life and career that are most important to me.

Money, title, and the prestige of the entity you work for all hold immense value in our society. There's nothing inherently wrong with desiring any of these elements as you build your career roadmap. The key, however, is to have a plan for your career and a vision of where you want it to take you in life.

Conclusion: 8 Tips For Building A Career Roadmap

1. Envision The Professional Life You Want

In your dream world, where do you envision yourself professionally five years from now? Zoom out a little further and imagine your ideal professional life ten years down the line. How about twenty years even? As you envision your dream work life, think big, because our world is full of endless possibilities. Corporate America has a way of causing us to sometimes shrink our dreams, so be mindful about only conjuring up positive thoughts. At this stage of your road mapping, only think about your destination. Don't worry yet about how you will get there. Just identify your dream professional life. Building a vision board is a great exercise for this stage in the process because it is a physical manifestation of what you envision for your life. The act of looking up images that reflect your vision and placing them on your board will provide clarity around what it is that you truly want.

2. Get In Tune With Your Motivational Needs

My stint at Goldman Sachs kickstarted a journey of self-reflection and evaluation. It made me realize that I wasn't really motivated by title or money. I was most motivated by having my purpose in life reflected in the work I do every day. Here's an exercise you can try to help you identify your motivational needs. Rank the following motivators on a scale of 1-10, with one being your strongest motivator and 10 being your weakest:

- Curiosity: There are plenty of things to investigate and think about
- Acceptance: The people around me approve of what I do and who I am
- Power: I'm able to influence what happens around me
- Relatedness: I have good social contacts with people in my work
- Goal: My purpose in life is reflected in the work that I do
- Honor: I feel proud that my personal values are reflected in how I work
- Mastery: My work challenges my competence, but it is still within my abilities
- Order: There are enough rules and policies in place for a stable environment
- Freedom: I am independent of others with my work and my responsibilities
- Status: My position is good and recognized by the people who work with me.

3. Nurture Your Imagination

What type of content are you ingesting every day? Are you a doom-scroller who spends excessive amounts of time on your phone following social media? Do you fall into wormholes of negative news stories or obsessively check your work email at all hours of the day and night? We live in a noisy world that is constantly bombarding us with garbage content from the minute we wake up to the minute we fall asleep. This type of noise can drown out your vocational calling. Instead of doomscrolling, watch movies. Believe it or not, the right types of films can open your mind to all sorts of possibilities and inspire you to take action to enhance your life. Another exercise that I love is throwing on my favorite music and daydreaming. I've found that the right type of music can transport you into another dimension of reality and can get you in touch with the desires of your subconscious mind. Indulging in art for a few minutes every day—regardless of the art form you engage in—will nourish your inner wisdom and voice and open your mind to all sorts of possibilities.

4. **Embrace The Adventure**

   It is so easy to just stay where you are and do the same things you've always done. It may even feel like the safer play. Comfort and familiarity certainly have their place in this life. But sometimes they can be an illusion. And in corporate America, the most dangerous place is to sit in your comfort zone. That vision you have for your life will require you to step out of your comfort zone to try something new. Prepare yourself mentally to take that first step. As you gear up for the journey, keep in mind a famous quote from Mark Twain:

   > *"Twenty years from now you will be more disappointed by the things you didn't do than by the ones you did do. So, throw off the bowlines. Sail away from the safe harbor. Catch the trade winds in your sails. Explore. Dream. Discover."*

If you embrace the adventure and follow what's calling you—you'll never be bored.

5. Build Your Plan

There's nothing complex about this stage of the process. Start by assessing where you're at and simply identify your dream destination. Next, pinpoint the obstacles you'll need to overcome to reach that destination. Your route is the path you'll take to conquer these obstacles and close the gap between where you are and where you're trying to go. As you build your plan, you'll need to identify attainable goals, along with a plan of attack for achieving them. (More on that next.)

6. Set Goals

Now comes the fun part. What steps are you taking at this very moment to make that dream professional life of yours a reality? Goal setting is a crucial element in this process. Your dream professional life is a big, fat whale. Don't worry about eating it all at once. Just take it one bite at a time. In this analogy, your goals are those bites at the whale. The whale is your overarching vision. Goals will motivate you as you work towards your vision. They'll provide you with purpose during the journey as well as a sense of accomplishment along the way. Goals will serve as a reminder that your vision doesn't have to be built in a day. Life doesn't work that way. It's all about process. Evolution is how this works—not through the snap of a finger. This reminds me of a 3,000 pushup challenge I once participated in as part of a fundraiser for cancer research on behalf of St. Jude's Children's Hospital. The idea was to do 3,000 pushups in a single month. At the time, the thought of doing even a few hundred pushups every day was too overwhelming for me to think about. So, I set a daily goal for pushup output during the workweek. I did 150 pushups a day Monday through Friday for four weeks. Within 30 days I'd achieved the overarching vision of 3,000 pushups for the month.

Setting goals is a deeply meaningful exercise in the process of actualizing your vision. As the actor Denzel Washington says: "Dreams without goals are just dreams, and ultimately, they fuel disappointment. On the way to achieving your dreams, you must apply discipline, but more importantly: consistency. Because without commitment, you'll never start. But without consistency, you'll never finish."

7. Recruit An Accountability Partner

Setting goals is one thing. Accomplishing those goals is another matter, and the journey towards reaching them is a lonely one. The process is grinding and staying motivated can be a challenge. An accountability partner is a critical resource who won't let you give up. They'll give you a Lionel Messi-like kick in the pants when you need one. To make this relationship an effective one, create a plan for regular check-ins to track your progress with your partner. This doesn't have to be a huge time commitment, either. Even check-ins over text can be effective. As human beings, we weren't made to survive alone, and you don't have to approach the work you're doing to make your dreams a reality that way. There isn't an exact science for choosing an accountability partner. The lone requirement is that they're committed to keeping you on track.

8. Persevere

"The people who stick with things for years and years and never stop almost always win the race."

—James Clear, author

"Everyone has a plan until they get punched in the mouth."

—Mike Tyson

You've identified your vision, embraced the adventure, formed a plan, set goals, and even recruited an accountability partner. Now comes the hard part. As you go on this journey, recognize that your endurance will be tested along the way. As surely as Monday follows Sunday, there will be setbacks throughout your journey. There will be people of influence in your way who will say, "No, it can't be done." Look for opportunities within the setbacks. Rethink your approach if necessary and be ready for change—because that is the only constant in this life. But whatever you do, never give up. The future you—the version of yourself that you dream of—depends on it.

CHAPTER FOUR

FITTING INTO THE CORPORATE CULTURE

"Fitting in is about assessing a situation and becoming who you need to be to be accepted. Belonging, on the other hand, doesn't require us to change who we are; it requires us to be who we are."

—Brené Brown

Following the 2013-14 NBA season, the Golden State Warriors made a baffling decision: they fired their head coach, Mark Jackson. To many NBA fans and observers at the time, the decision seemed like a questionable one. Over three years, Jackson had transformed a mediocre NBA team into a squad that seemed to be a step or two away from championship contention. Under Jackson's leadership, the team had just enjoyed its first 50-win season in nineteen years, and they were coming off a second consecutive playoff appearance in the NBA's difficult Western Conference.

So, what went wrong for Mark Jackson during his time with the Golden State Warriors? Why did the Warriors ownership decide to part ways with him after two consecutive playoff appearances, a

121-109 record, and a proven track record of developing multiple young talents on the roster into perennial all-stars?

Based on the detailed reports that emerged from numerous news outlets in the weeks and months following the firing, it is clear that Jackson failed to succeed at the very thing that all careers live and die on: one's ability to fit into the organizational culture.

Warriors' owner, Joe Lacob, when speaking at a luncheon the month after Jackson's firing to a group of venture capitalists confirmed the news outlet's conclusions. Before the firing, Jackson had resisted Lacob's suggestion that he should recruit new assistant coaches. Jackson also reportedly had dysfunctional relationships throughout the organization, even with a number of his hand-picked assistant coaches. Jackson would go weeks, for example, without even speaking to his top assistant, Mike Malone.

Speaking about Jackson and his successor, Steve Kerr, to a group of venture capitalists in late 2014, Lacob said:

"Look, he did a great job, and I'll always compliment him in many respects, but you can't have 200 people in the organization dislike you."

The curious case of Mark Jackson's failed coaching career with the Golden State Warriors is instructive for Black men in any corporate environment. More than a decade after his firing, Jackson has yet to land another coaching job in the NBA and is considered by many league observers to have been blackballed from the profession.

To succeed in the corporate world, which I'm defining as any office environment where your actions are accountable to more than one person, fitting into the culture is mission critical.

According to the Society for Human Resource Management (SHRM), "an organization's culture consists of shared beliefs and values established by leaders, and then communicated and reinforced" in various ways that shape employee perceptions, behaviors, and understanding. The most successful companies (and NBA teams) possess strong organizational cultures, and the employees who thrive in these environments are those who succeed at bringing the culture to life through their work.

For Black executives and corporate professionals, while fitting into corporate culture is not necessarily about race or suppressing personal beliefs or values, it does come with its own set of unique stressors and challenges. To be Black in corporate America means you're unlikely to see any senior leaders who look like you. If you're more junior or mid-level in your career, you may also be one of the few among the rank-and-file. (This was the case for me for the first thirteen years of my career. I got used to being one of the few of us in the room.) Because of this, we as Black professionals must perform a delicate balancing act in maintaining our authentic identities while fitting into organizational cultures that are shaped and influenced by the racial majority.

Early in my financial services career, I learned an important lesson about what it means to be a cultural fit within an organization. After spending my first eight years out of college as a journalist, I decided to transition into financial services. The news business was in the midst of a massive transition from the traditional print and broadcast-based approach to a digital, social-media-driven model that brought with it a constant stream of rapid-fire headlines and a news cycle that had expanded to 24 hours a day, seven days a week.

In search of a change of pace and better upside earning potential, I took a job writing news features for the company-wide intranet site at a major, Boston-based investment firm. The role represented a foot in the door for me within the finance industry, and it taught me how to begin thinking like a marketer. It was a junior role, but it was a transformative experience that led to incredible successes down the line. The main purpose of that position was to create content that would get employees jazzed up about investing in the firm's products and services. The idea was that if we could convince 40,000+ employees to engage with the firm's offerings, they'd tell friends and family about them, and ultimately help the company grow its customer base.

To land the job, I had to take an early-morning flight up to Boston from New York to meet several executives who'd make the final call on whether to bring me into the firm. I was so nervous about the last round of interviews that during the drive to La Guardia Airport, I had the cab driver pull over on the shoulder of the Long Island Expressway so I could throw up. I had a lot riding on landing this position. My wife and I had a nine-month-old baby at home. She wasn't working at the time, and my instincts told me there were layoffs on the horizon at my current employer. In addition to my desire to get out of the news business entirely, job prospects throughout the media industry weren't too promising in the post-2008 market environment.

To my pleasant surprise, I found the team at that investment firm to be warm, welcoming, and genuinely interested in what I had to offer as a candidate. All the executives I met with were White, but the lack of diversity on display didn't bother me at that moment because of the connections I was able to forge during the interview process. I even saw my race as an asset at the time and I remember thinking to myself: "They *need* people like me at this firm. And I *know* that they know that!"

However, one thing did stand out for me during that final round of interviews. The woman who would eventually become my manager walked me towards the exit. As we made light chit-chat, she said something that stuck with me.

"We all feel really good about getting the chance to meet you and I already know you made a nice impression on the team. I think we all see you as a cultural fit here."

I recall smiling at the remark but after we said our goodbyes and I headed to Logan Airport for the trip home, I kept thinking to myself: "Wait, what?" For weeks after that, and well into my first months in the role, I ruminated on that remark. What exactly did she mean that I was a "cultural fit" for the firm?

I gained some clarity into the meaning of cultural fit several weeks into the job when I learned the backstory of why the role was even available in the first place. My predecessor, who happened to have been an Ivy League-educated White man, had routinely alienated business partners with the way he went about doing the job. Our role was to raise awareness of product offerings and to create content strategies aimed at engaging and informing employees about key developments around the firm.

It was pretty vanilla stuff, and frankly, it was the type of role that any person with a sense of ambition would quickly outgrow after a year or two. But it was also the type of role that brought significant exposure to leaders and colleagues across various lines of business, which meant that it was a gateway to greater opportunity at the company if you played your cards right.

Well, this guy played his cards terribly wrong. He was fired because he treated the role as if he were a tabloid reporter who was chasing scoops. He took an overly aggressive approach to the work, which alienated one too many business partners. After months of pissing people off left and right, he was eventually fired.

Like most banks, investment shops, and brokerage firms, this investment firm's employee base and leadership population is overwhelmingly White. But in this case, I was a cultural fit for the place-based largely on how I approached my work, whereas my White predecessor was not. I treated my internal product collaborators as clients and took a "customer is always right" approach to the work. I made them feel that my win was their win and that their opinions mattered.

Despite occupying positions that were worlds apart both economically and in terms of the platform they offer, both my predecessor and Mark Jackson held several unfortunate traits in common. For starters, their approach to the work alienated their colleagues. This led to strained relationships in their organizations, which negatively impacted their ability to be effective in their roles. They also didn't adhere to the vision for their roles as laid out by their bosses. This made both men expendable when push came to shove.

The Role of Race in American Corporate Culture

"You're a Black guy in Boston. You don't need any help from me to be completely fucked."

—Billy Costigan
(played by Leonardo DiCaprio in The Departed.)

The investment firm is headquartered in Boston, and I felt fortunate that I wouldn't have to uproot my young family and move there for the role. Instead, I was able to do the job from a small office across the street from Rockefeller Center in New York. Within the universe of the New England-centric company, midtown Manhattan was an outpost, which didn't bother me one bit. Although face time at the home office was critical for relationship building and career progression, I was more than fine with a job arrangement that would only require me to travel to Boston every few months.

That small midtown office also happened to be a rare bastion of diversity within the company. There were five Black people that I knew of among the thousands who worked at the company—and three of them worked alongside me in that Rockefeller Center office. They became some of my closest friends at the firm, and I was thankful for the safe space they provided me to vent my frustrations, share laughs, enjoy some happy hours, and recap our favorite shows—which at the time were *Game of Thrones* and *Breaking Bad*.

To be perfectly honest with you, I was afraid of the city of Boston, and to a lesser extent, even the company's headquarters as well! Looking back, I realize that I'd internalized Boston's reputation as one of America's most racist cities and carried that perception of the city with me on every trip to the company's waterfront office building. In hindsight though, I realize that this perspective was crippling, and it prevented me from finding joy in the opportunity or having fun hanging out in what really is a beautiful city.

As a die-hard sports fan, I first became aware of Boston's reputation through countless reports from Black athletes[44] and journalists[45] who said that Boston was the only place they had ever been called the N-word. I also recalled stories from elders about the violence that Black children faced in 1974 when a U.S. District Judge ordered the busing of Black students to predominantly White schools. Fresh against the backdrop of the Civil Rights Movement, Boston's busing riots shocked the country. Black students were met by angry crowds who threw bricks, bottles, and eggs at their buses as they tried to go to school.[46]

Compounding matters for me was the fact that I rarely saw Black people represented at any level at the company's headquarters. Sure, I saw Black people driving buses in Boston and working at the Dunkin Donuts and the other shops and restaurants at South Station. But among the population of white-collar professionals at that firm, they were few and far between during my time there.

Back in the spring of 2012, I received an opportunity to attend the company's full-day senior leadership forum in Boston. To be in those rooms, to rub elbows with senior leaders all day and connect with them over food and drinks that evening was a rare privilege that most employees could only dream of. But there wasn't a single Black leader attending that event or participating in any of the panel discussions or presentations. I was the only Black attendee at that leadership forum (and a junior-level employee to boot). It was an incredibly isolating experience. By the end of that day, my face was sore from all the forced smiles I felt I needed to put on, and I was emotionally

---

[44] Tori Hunter Details Racist Encounters that led to Boston No-Trade Clause, June 9, 2020
[45] Michael Wilbon: Boston Only Place I've Been Called the N-Word to My Face, June 11, 2020
[46] History Channel, Feb. 9, 2010

Company Men

drained from wearing a mask of charm that I saw as necessary to help me fit in with my colleagues.

Now, don't get me wrong. I made a ton of close friends at the company during my tenure, and I look back with great respect for what they've built and how they serve their clients. That company, in my opinion, is one of the most solid firms in the industry and they take great pains to invest in their employees. Their 401(k) is second to none in my humble opinion.

But let's also confront the uncomfortable truth. And this goes far beyond my tenure at that Boston-based investment shop. The vast majority of financial services firms simply aren't diverse, and there are clear historical reasons for this. For example, *New York Times* reporter Emily Flitter notes in her 2022 book: "*The White Wall: How Big Finance Bankrupts Black America*," that the big brokerage houses in the mid-and late twentieth century simply did not hire or promote Black workers.[47] The mandate for these shops was to grow wealth for their predominantly White clientele, and they were led and staffed by employees who reflected the communities they served. The banking sector was no different. Today, largely as a result of this history, Black workers account for just 7.9 percent of professional workers in the banking industry and hold less than 4 percent of top managerial roles.[48]

The numbers are just as bad beyond the financial services industry. Despite the renewed focus from U.S. corporations on diversity, equity, and inclusion following the tragic events of 2020, Black workers remain heavily concentrated in dead-end jobs within lower-paying service industries and are woefully underrepresented in higher-paying corporate roles in growth industries.[49] In its 2021

---

[47] The White Wall: How Big Finance Corrupts Black America, 2022
[48] Morning Brew, 8 Charts that Explore Racial Disparities in the Banking Industry, May 18, 2021
[49] McKinsey Global Institute, "Race in the workplace: The Black experience in the US private sector, Feb. 21, 2021

report, "Race in the Workplace: The Black Experience in the US Private Sector," the McKinsey Global Institute notes that three in five Black workers work in frontline jobs such as service workers, laborers, operatives, and office and clerical workers. Conversely, McKinsey notes, there continues to be a dearth of Black workers in higher-wage, high-growth industries like informational technology or professional services.

I receive grim reminders of this every day on trips to grab lunch or coffee, where the servers are usually persons of color – often Latino or Black – while most of the folks who are being served are not. Despite my small crew of Black colleagues at our Manhattan company outpost, I went to work every day against the backdrop of severely limited diversity at all levels of the company. Succeeding there required that I get comfortable with being uncomfortable. I carried with me an implicit awareness that to fit in and build a career there, I would need to do two things: 1) Be really, *really* good at my job. I needed to shine and be so good at the work that no one could pick it apart. 2) Disarm people with charm and likability. Based on what I'd observed, I may have been the first Black colleague some of my peers ever had. Finding acceptance within that environment, both personally and professionally, was crucial. Unfortunately for me, that would be easier said than done.

Code-switching: A Necessary Evil

"Hey, young blood. Let me give you a tip. Use your white voice."

—Langston
(played by Danny Glover in the film,
Sorry to Bother You.)

Growing up, I always found it oddly amusing that whenever I called my mom at work, usually for the express purpose of borrowing money, she would answer the phone with a distinct voice. I wouldn't say it was a "White" voice, but it was certainly a different tone than the one she used at home. It was a restrained, professional-sounding voice that was unlike how she would speak in less formal settings. I'd liken her work voice to the vocal equivalent of someone being in a straitjacket.

My mom spent most of her 30-year career as an executive assistant at prestigious white-shoe firms like Goldman Sachs and Brown Brothers Harriman, and the voice she used when answering my calls reflected the cultures in which she worked. Throughout the middle of the twentieth century, such companies were the exclusive domain of the East Coast, White Anglo-Saxon Protestant elite. The leaders and employees at these firms were predominantly men who were the product of Ivy League educations, and as Investopedia notes: they were "as white as the shoes they wore on weekends at their country clubs, many of which refused to admit Jews, Catholics, or people of color.[50]"

These types of companies were almost entirely inaccessible to Black, Jewish, and other minority talent throughout much of the twentieth century, and even as many began to open their doors to more diverse talent in the latter decades of the 1900s, they still reflected the cultural DNA of their roots. During my tenures at such firms as Goldman Sachs and JPMorgan Chase, I'd often think to myself how fortunate I was to be working in a period when skin color couldn't prevent me from rising into the executive ranks at such places. But on the other side of that coin, I also carried the knowledge that had I been born a few decades earlier, the best I could probably have hoped for in such companies would be to clean the offices, shine the shoes, or serve the lunch. Former U.S. president Bill Clinton served up a nasty reminder of this reality when speaking of Barack Obama during the 2008 Democratic presidential primary,

---

[50] Source: Investopedia: June 25, 2022

he allegedly told Sen. Ted Kennedy: "A few years ago this guy would have been getting us coffee.⁵¹"

The Civil Rights Movement helped to knock down the historical barriers to entry on Wall Street and corporate America in the 1970s. But the cultures that had been established at these shops were deeply ingrained. If you were Black and working at one of these firms, trying to fit in, you almost certainly deployed the technique that sociologists have dubbed code-switching.

As Harvard Business Review notes: "Code-switching involves adjusting one's style of speech, appearance, behavior, and expression in ways that will optimize the comfort of others in exchange for fair treatment, quality service, and employment opportunities.⁵²"

Simply put, people code-switch so that those in the majority will treat them with respect and afford them the same opportunities and courtesies they'd provide to anyone else. Within corporate settings, many people of color feel a need to talk, dress, and behave like the majority to be accepted by that majority as equals, much less as leaders.

Growing up in working-class, predominantly Black, pre-gentrification Brooklyn during the late 1980s and 1990s, I first learned about code-switching from the pastor of our church, the Rev. Dr. Fred Lucas of Bridge Street AME, which is in the historic Bedford-Stuyvesant neighborhood. When I was 14 or 15, he delivered a talk to our male teen group about how we would need to be "culturally bilingual" to find acceptance both on the streets of Brooklyn, and with our teachers at school and eventually colleagues at work. Most of us already knew this implicitly, but Rev. Lucas was the first person who clearly articulated to me the challenge we were facing.

There were certain norms you had to adhere to if you wanted to be able to maneuver through the neighborhood and be accepted

---

⁵¹ Teddy's Anger, Politico, Jan 9, 2010
⁵² Harvard Business Review: "The Costs of Code-Switching, Nov. 15, 2019"

socially. In a similar fashion to how I had to contort myself to fit into corporate America, finding acceptance socially as a young Black man where I grew up required that you walked a certain way, talked a certain way, and dressed a certain way. You had to carry yourself with a swagger that commanded respect. The sneakers you wore had to be on point, and you couldn't be dressed like some Banana Republic preppy. For young Black men, Starter jackets, JanSport bookbags, professional sports apparel, and Guess Jeans were the uniform. The dialect was Brooklyn slang, and you had to be able to hold your own physically. That meant being proficient at everything from playing basketball and football to being able to outdo your peers in the mandatory slap-boxing matches that could break out at a moment's notice. (These matches could also spill over into full-fledged fights as well, and getting your ass kicked was a ticket to losing the respect of your peers.)

Meanwhile, the scholastic world required a different set of skills. Despite a brief rough patch academically, I spent most of my upbringing in gifted programs and even took Advanced Placement classes in high school. It didn't take a genius to recognize that the social and physical skills that I needed to leverage on the streets had no place in the classroom. For those of us who would venture off into corporate America, school was a great social training ground. This was the place to speak proper, Will Smith-style English and to comport yourself in a manner that would gain the respect of your teachers. Of course, this also came at a cost. I got razzed quite a bit growing up for the sin of supposedly trying to sound White when speaking in academic settings.

This experience with "cultural bilingualism" brings to mind the double consciousness that Black people deploy to find acceptance as Americans, which W.E.B DuBois describes in his seminal 1903 tome, *The Souls of Black Folk: Essays and Sketches*. DuBois' famous work describes the arduous tightrope Black people must traverse in balancing our dual identities as both Black people and as Americans. Although this work was published more than 120 years ago, we continue to grapple with the challenge of finding a place of comfort and peace within a fragmented identity while gaining full acceptance as insiders within American society.

During my time at that Boston-based investment firm, I'd joke with friends about the effort it took to code-switch at work. I called myself the Black Daniel Day-Lewis and likened myself to the acclaimed actor because of the method of acting[53] performances that I felt I needed to put on day after day to fit in. From the forced charm and smiles to the freshly-shaved face, the Brooks Brothers outfits, and the dulcet tones I spoke with—I saw myself as playing a character in a sense. This approach to work was twice as hard as that of my White colleagues, because I essentially was doing two jobs, whereas they only needed to perform one. I had to *work* to be the corporate version of myself *and* perform my role on top of that. Needless to say, it was an exhausting existence putting myself into character day after day—mentally, physically, and emotionally.

To work in corporate America demands the assimilation of everyone who participates, regardless of race. However, many corporate cultures are rooted in the social norms that were established in the mid-1900s when people of color had no place in such environments. Being professional meant conforming to the norms and mannerisms that were established by upper-class White men. You had to dress and behave in a way that was socially acceptable within the framework that the most dominant members of our society had established.

Despite the lack of representation at any level during my time at the Boston-based investment firm (aside from my New York colleagues,) I never saw my race as a barrier to success within the company. But I also had it in the back of my mind that I couldn't be too Black, either. I had to dilute who I was in some respects. For me, this meant taking some of the natural baritone out of my voice and suppressing the Brooklyn twang that's part of my normal manner

---

[53] Method Acting: A Performer's Guide, May 12, 2022

of speaking. Despite my preference for a beard, I booked weekly appointments at the barber shop to keep my facial hair in check while maintaining a crisp hairline. I also conformed more than I care to admit to the fashion sensibilities of my colleagues and adopted a conservative look befitting a man who worked at a New England-based financial services firm.

Overall, despite being a child of working-class Brooklyn, I felt that I had to reflect through my day-to-day behavior not just the blue blood culture of the company, but also the upper-middle-class mannerisms of my predominantly White peers. None of this came naturally to me, and the guys I grew up with would have barely recognized the character I found myself playing day after day.

But like most people of color working in corporate settings, I saw three key reasons why I felt I needed to do this. As was noted in the *Harvard Business Review*[54]:

1. "For black people and other racial minorities, downplaying membership in a stigmatized racial group helps increase perceptions of professionalism and the likelihood of being hired.
2. Avoiding negative stereotypes associated with black racial identity (e.g., incompetence, laziness) helps black employees be seen as leaders.
3. Expressing shared interests with members of dominant groups promotes similarity with powerful organizational members, which raises the chance of promotions because individuals tend to affiliate with people they perceive as similar."

Spending most of the waking hours of your life code-switching comes at a cost, however. Beyond the psychological tax of getting into character, deep down, part of you feels like a phony for operating this way. Research also shows that faking your way through work in

---

[54] The Costs of Code Switching, Harvard Business Review, Nov. 15, 2019

the name of finding common ground with your colleagues contributes to workplace fatigue and even burnout over time.[55] This is far beyond the vocal straitjacket I felt my mom used when she answered my calls to her office line. It's more like a psychological prison that ultimately prevents you from unleashing your full capabilities at work.

Embracing Your Blackness at Work with Tact

For people of color, *some* level of code-switching will always be necessary in settings where you're in both the racial and social minority. The key for Black talent, however, is to strike a balance between doing what it takes to fit in without fully losing the core of who you are in the process. That duality of identity that DuBois speaks of in *The Souls of Black Folk* will always be with us as Black Americans. Finding peace within this dual identity is the goal we must continually strive towards—especially when working in corporate America.

This requires a deft balancing act that the show *Key & Peele* hilariously depicts in the now-famous sketch *Meet & Greet,* which captures how President Obama code-switched during his eight years in the White House. Throughout his presidency, Obama had been known to alter the cadence and linguistic style of his speech depending on whether he was speaking to audiences that were predominantly White or Black. The *Key & Peele* sketch illustrates how the president "turned on his 'I'm one of you, charms' when the situation called for it while adhering strictly to the Queen's English when in front of White audiences."[56]

There's an ease to how Obama maneuvered between both worlds that I'm sure stems from the fact that he's biracial. Nevertheless, it's something that I've worked to emulate, and it's helped me navigate

---

[55] The Costs of Code Switching, Harvard Business Review, Nov. 15, 2019
[56] Key And Peele's Hilarious Take On Obama's Code Switching, NewsOne, Sept. 26, 2014

my career as I've climbed the ranks at some of America's largest, most influential companies.

As a new father during my days at the Boston-based firm, I also came to the realization that I had adopted a disempowered perspective when it comes to race. This was not something I wanted to pass on to my children. I wanted them to grow up *knowing* that they could be anything they envisioned and that if race caused some unexpected barrier to a goal they were striving to achieve, they would simply overcome it.

No matter your race, if you work in corporate America, you're going to have to blend into the culture of your company. Each firm has its own distinct culture that governs everything from how people dress, to how they work, how colleagues interact, and how success is defined. The one common denominator to it all is professionalism. Are you turning in quality work? And how are you making people feel in the process of getting the job done? As we've seen with both Mark Jackson and my predecessor at that investment firm, how you go about doing your job and interacting with colleagues matters just as much as the results.

Conclusion: 5 Tips for Black Men on How to Fit Within Mostly White Corporate Cultures

1. **Master The Art Of Being Likable**

    It is a simple fact of American life that we will spend a large chunk of our adult lives working. The author Annie Dillard put this into perspective when she said that: "How we spend our days, is of course how we spend our lives." Research shows that the average person will spend 90,000 hours at work throughout a lifetime.[57] That adds up to nearly one-third of your life. You will spend more hours during the

---

[57] One-third of your life is spent at work, Gettysburg University, Nov. 2022

work week interacting with coworkers than with your loved ones.

Spending this amount of time with people you genuinely like makes passing this time more enjoyable. But just as we have no control over the family we're born into, we have little control over the cards we're dealt when it comes to who our colleagues will be. Sometimes we simply get stuck working with people we don't like. It happens. But likability is a two-way street and mastering the art of being likable can help you develop friendships, build a network, and even be seen as an indispensable resource at the office. Above all, humans are social animals, and everyone—no matter their race, gender, or religion—wants to be liked. It's a universal need. I've deployed several techniques to be seen as likable at work by peers and leaders, including:

- Put genuine effort into getting to know your colleagues. This means moving beyond the small talk and investing time in getting to know people. If you work at a large firm, this can seem daunting, but finding three to five people within your orbit to start with can help.

- Bring a good attitude to work every day. Early in my financial services career, there was a colleague on our team whose moods would vary greatly from day to day. At times, this person could be as bright and sunny as a beautiful spring day. On other occasions, they'd bring a dark and downright unpleasant attitude to the office and would genuinely not be someone you'd enjoy being around. Despite being a talented person, over time I saw them written off by both their teammates and management.

- Be helpful—and seek help when you need it. Believe it or not, we're actually programmed by evolution to feel better about the people that we help, as well as the people who help us.[58] Seek out opportunities to lend a helping hand to colleagues or leaders in need. Over time, this will help you to build trust with co-workers, which is the bedrock of any strong relationship—be it personal or professional.

2. **Become A Superstar At Your Job.**
   - To fit into your corporate culture, it helps to be a strong performer. But as a Black American, it's important to take a healthy approach to that. It's not about feeling that you have to work yourself to death or be constantly in a state of competition with your colleagues. Instead, pour your focus into mastering your craft—whatever it is. This will go a long way towards gaining you professional respect over time. When combined with the right relationships, being good at what you do will even carry you to new heights over time. Most companies today do recognize the need for more diversity—not just among the rank-and-file, but also within their leadership. Becoming a superstar employee will carry you further in your career than you might expect.

3. **Don't be like Larry David—Develop Your Emotional Intelligence.**
   - The long-running HBO series *Curb Your Enthusiasm* centers on the misadventures of Larry David, who repeatedly finds himself in uncomfortable social situations due to an utter and complete lack of emotional intelligence. He has a comical lack of understanding or care for how his words and actions are perceived by others. In real life,

---

[58] 7 Easy Ways to Become More Likable at Work, Inc. Magazine, June 25, 2015

David wouldn't last five minutes in corporate America. His character on the show, which is based on his real-life experience as the creator of Seinfeld, is also independently wealthy and essentially free to behave like an asshole. Most of us don't have that luxury. Our livelihood and reputation depend in large part on our ability to get along with others. When combined with strong work performance, mastering your emotional intelligence—which is defined as the capacity to be aware of, control, and express your emotions, and to handle interpersonal relationships judiciously and empathetically—can put you on a long-term path toward the corner office. Those who fail at this core skill run the risk of alienating colleagues and ultimately finding themselves marginalized at work, or even worse.

4. **Embrace The Duality Of Black American Life**
- In today's multicultural society, there are no limits to the opportunities available if you're a person of color. But within the corporate world, the simple fact remains that although there's never been a better time than now to be credentialed, talented, and Black, you will have to comport yourself in a manner befitting a professional if you're going to succeed in corporate America. Every person of color code-switches at some level. One thing that I've found that helps is finding a role model who deftly manages to navigate that balance between being their authentic self while blending into a predominantly White corporate culture. Take queues from them. It's also important to find your tribe within the firm. I mentioned earlier that finding three to five people at the company to build genuine relationships with helps. Lean on this network as a safe space where you can let your guard down as well. Code-switching is draining, but trusted relationships within your

company can help recharge your batteries and allow you to find some balance. Being able to let your guard down with a few trusted colleagues will also provide you with a safe space to be your authentic self.

5. Feel Empowered About Your Race—Even If You're The Only One In The Room.

- Being the only Black person in the room is never easy. Personally, I've found that it brings with it a heightened sense of "otherness" that can be so stifling it can choke out the gifts and abilities that made you an attractive hire in the first place. It's hard to excel at work when you don't feel comfortable about being there. Joining an employee resource group can help in this regard. "Employee resource groups—also known as ERGs, affinity groups, or business resource groups—are affiliated subgroups of employees within an organization who share distinctive qualities, interests, or goals. They have historically organized around gender and race, and many companies have ERGs representing the LGBTQ and veteran communities.[59]" Most companies deploy ERGs to foster inclusion and today, 90% of all Fortune 500 firms have ERGs.[60] Beyond that, embrace the fact that no company today wants to be seen as racist or inhospitable to Black or other talent of color. You were hired for a reason—because you are good at what you do. Otherwise, you wouldn't be there.

---

[59] 90% Of Fortune 500 Companies Already Have A Solution To Gender Equality But Aren't Utilizing It, Forbes, Nov. 13, 2017

[60] 90% Of Fortune 500 Companies Already Have A Solution To Gender Equality But Aren't Utilizing It, Forbes, Nov. 13, 2017

CHAPTER FIVE

WHEN TO STAND ON YOUR CONVICTIONS AND WHEN TO LET GO

"You must never be fearful about what you are doing when it is right."

—Rosa Parks

After two decades in corporate America, I've learned that one of the keys to long-term success (and survival) is knowing the hills that are worth dying on. You've got to develop a sixth sense about the battles that are worth fighting, versus when to concede and move on.

You can certainly gain valuable lessons from losing a battle—but you don't want to take too many L's (losses) in the corporate world. It's not a good look for your personal brand or your psyche. So, as a rule, I only fight battles that I know deep down I can win. And when it's not clear that a battle is winnable, I either concede and move on, or bide my time until a better moment to strike presents itself.

Understanding this distinction between when to take a stand and when to concede can help you earn the respect of the people who matter in your organization. It will help you to understand when it's time to walk away from a company and open a new chapter. It can even play a role in setting you up for a leadership position in the future because it demonstrates the good judgment, sober thinking, and boldness that are required for top jobs.

But most importantly, knowing when to stand on your convictions will help you to keep your integrity intact, and not lose the core of who you are— no matter where you work, or what your position may be.

I learned the lesson of understanding when it's time to fight and when to back down long before I ever set foot in a corporate office. It's something I learned in the school of hard knocks, on a Brooklyn schoolyard in what feels like another life—back when I was in the seventh grade.

My lesson began on a warm, sunny morning in the spring of 1993, when I got into a silly argument with one of my classmates—a dude named Marvin Lee.

Before that fateful day, Marvin and I were cool with each other. Not the best of friends, but we were in the same lunchroom crew, and we respected each other's athletic abilities so much that we usually picked each other when choosing sides for schoolyard basketball and touch football games. Where I'm from, this was one of the highest forms of respect one adolescent boy could demonstrate to a peer.

But for some reason, we found ourselves at odds on this memorable morning. Whatever we were arguing about was so stupid I no longer remember the root cause of it decades later. But unfortunately for us, there were some instigators nearby who began egging us on to fight as our argument heated up. With those instigators throwing gasoline on an open fire, the tension between Marvin and I built up to the point where we began exchanging hostile words to each other's faces. Eventually, we found ourselves nose-to-nose, the way boxers do at a weigh-in before a fight.

Fortunately, Marvin and I were saved by the homeroom bell before a single punch was thrown. But as we separated to make our way to our respective homeroom classes, we agreed to settle the matter after school with a good 'ole fistfight in the yard at three o'clock.

As the day progressed, news of the upcoming fight spread throughout the entire school, which consisted of grades six through eight. At every grade level, it seemed like the fight was all anyone cared about. For hundreds of students—boys and girls alike—the bout between Marvin and I was the day's headline. The atmosphere at the Dyker Heights Junior High School that day was reminiscent of what it was like on the day of a Mike Tyson fight —back when Tyson was a vicious knockout artist at the height of his powers. In the hours before a Tyson fight in the early 1990s, you knew something violent was about to go down, with the tension gradually rising as time marched forward towards the opening bell.

And on this memorable school day, as the clock ticked away, minute by minute, and morning gave way to afternoon, nervous excitement pulsated throughout the entire student body.

To that point, I'd been a veteran of a few schoolyard tussles. I'd won some and lost some, but I'd never experienced anything like this—where a schoolyard fight I was headlining would take place in front of a horde of kids. The growing frenzy throughout the school put my inner voice on high alert, and I sensed that something far more dangerous than your standard schoolyard fisticuffs was about to go down.

At three o'clock, the final bell of the day rang. With not a single adult anywhere in sight, a huge chunk of our student body—damn near 100 students—made its way to the yard. Eventually, Marvin and I found ourselves encircled by a mob. A palpable bloodlust filled the air, and I handed my glasses over to one of the instigators for safekeeping ahead of the fight.

As the mob waited for me or Marvin to throw the first punch, I felt in the pit of my stomach that the two of us were in grave danger. I feared being trampled beneath that mob or that a full-on riot could pop off. (Adding to my fears was that there was zero doubt some of the thugs in that crowd were armed with blades, knives, and brass knuckles and were itching for a reason to use them.)

As I looked to Marvin's right, I saw a boy with a crazed, manic look in his eyes. With his teeth flashing a wild grin, he rapidly pumped his clenched fists up and down with excitement, waiting for the action to begin.

At this point, my inner voice said to me, "Why are you doing this? To impress that crazy motherfucker? Or those dudes who egged you on to this point? Are you ready to put your life in danger for these fools? Is this a fight worth dying for?"

To make matters worse, I couldn't even remember why I was so angry at Marvin in the first place. I felt like a fool because at that moment I realized I'd allowed myself to be pulled into a dangerous place by outside forces, and not because I had genuine conviction about fighting this battle (which my heart wasn't in.)

As these thoughts raced through my mind, I found myself alone in the midst of a mob that was hungry for violence. I was also grappling with those age-old pressures that begin in adolescence and never fully go away (especially if you work in the corporate world): the desire to fit in with the crowd, be respected, accepted, and not be the object of gossip, scorn, or second-guessing.

But at that moment, I concluded that the risks that came with throwing the first punch far outweighed the meager rewards of giving the blood-thirsty crowd the action they craved.

As Marvin and I stared each other down, I decided I didn't need to prove anything to these people. It wasn't worth it. I knew at that moment that if Marvin didn't throw the first punch and give me a clear, obvious reason to defend myself, I wasn't going to fight.

After a tense few minutes of waiting for Marvin to attempt the first blow—and with the mob hooting, hollering, and growing antsy, I turned to one of the instigators and said: "Gimme my glasses." After putting them back on, I walked away from a fight I had zero conviction in participating in.

The mile-long walk from my school to the B train for the ride home was one of the longest, loneliest walks of my childhood. In that moment, and in the days to come, I was razzed as a coward, punk, and a few other harsh names by some of the instigators and tough guys throughout the school.

I didn't realize it at the time, but that experience was a blessing in disguise. It made me immune to being pressured into making decisions that I didn't believe in—no matter who was pushing me. It also gave me a thicker skin, which is another requirement for making difficult decisions when the stakes are high, and the world is watching.

Within a week, the whole episode was pretty much forgotten, but the lesson from it has lasted a lifetime.[61] It taught me the importance of standing up for what you believe in—even when you're under pressure from powerful outside forces who are trying to compel you to do things that don't align with your instincts, beliefs, or values. That experience taught me it's important to trust your instincts when the time comes to make crucial decisions—even if other people don't share your vision in the moment (and might even talk badly about you later on.)

This is a lesson that would serve me well decades later, during my time in the corporate world both as a junior-level employee and as an executive. It helped me to develop the stiff backbone and steely resolve that are necessary when the time comes to make difficult choices that will impact business outcomes—and the lives of others.

Sometimes, walking away from a battle is the right thing to do. But on other occasions, there will be moments when you've got to stand firm. Even if it puts you at odds with a superior.

---

[61] My reputation actually recovered, thanks in large part due to my athletic abilities. In a sweet coincidence, there was a school-wide intramural touch football tournament a few days after I walked away from that fight. And during that week-long tournament, I quarterbacked a team of nerds, social misfits, and castoffs to the championship—even defeating a few of the dudes who razzed me as a coward along the way.

You don't need permission to do the right thing

"You have enemies? Good. That means you've stood up for something, sometime in your life."

—Winston Churchill

In the weeks and months before the COVID-19 pandemic exploded onto the world stage, I was on the road for work—a LOT. In any given month, I could be anywhere in the country for days or weeks at a time, overseeing company activations or attending meetings with clients, community partners, and sometimes, even the press. I'd gotten used to living out of a suitcase, staying at the finest hotels, and of course, using little hacks to secure flight upgrades by any means necessary. Although I hated all the time that work required me to be away from my wife (and two young children) I loved that all this travel helped me to rack up frequent flier miles that I'd use to splurge on spring- and summer-break trips with my family.

But at my core, I'm a family man—which meant that the constant travel was never ideal. It was simply a means to an end—a necessary sacrifice for me to provide the best possible lifestyle I could afford for my family.

In Feb. 2020, I came across an article in The Atlantic about a frightening new coronavirus that was rapidly spreading in China— which one scientist predicted would infect up to 70% of the world's population.[62] I spent the next few weeks paying close attention to any news I could find about this new virus— knowing that all the time I spent on the road put me at a heightened risk of exposure if this bug turned into a full-on outbreak like that scientist predicted.

Towards the end of February, it was becoming clear it was only a matter of time before COVID-19 tore through the U.S. population,

---

[62] You're Likely to Get the Coronavirus. The Atlantic, Feb. 24, 2020

and I felt a growing unease about a series of large-scale events my company had planned at Disney World in early March.

I recognized early on that traveling to the Orlando theme park, which attracts millions of visitors from around the world every month, presented a major public health risk that would not only potentially jeopardize my health—but also the health of my team, our CEO, and most importantly, my family.

For weeks before the trip, I'd pepper our senior leadership with the same question:

"Are we really proceeding with this? Are we going to do it?" And every time, I'd get the same answer, some version of: "'Just hang on. We're not ready to make the call yet. Let's wait to see if Disney will cancel first.'"

With two days to go before my team, CEO, and I were scheduled to travel to Orlando, I decided to take matters into my own hands. I made a unilateral decision to contact Disney myself and cancel our planned events.

The reaction from my superior on the project was ugly. "How dare you do this? I've got to protect the company and our reputation," she snarled over the phone. "This was not your call to make."

This was the first time in my career I was on the receiving end of a loud tongue-lashing by a senior leader. And it wouldn't be the last in the tumultuous days of March 2020. (I was reprimanded that same week for telling my manager I'd be working from home indefinitely, without asking for the company's permission.)

My decisive actions were soon vindicated, even as tensions simmered between senior leadership and me. On the day we were supposed to travel to Orlando, the World Health Organization declared COVID-19 a global pandemic. The following day, Disney closed its parks due to the outbreak. The lockdown, and our company's order to work from home, came shortly after that.

By the beginning of March 2020, I knew that proceeding with our series of activations at Disney World would be the absolute wrong thing to do and that there was no way I was getting on a plane to Orlando—or putting our company in jeopardy by allowing our CEO to do so, either. I saw this as a winnable battle that was worth fighting. I was a strong performer and knew that all the leadership team could do at that moment was get angry. Nothing more. In this case, I knew I had all the leverage, and that the worst that would happen was a loud slap on the wrist.

By the end of March 2020, with the U.S. in full lockdown mode, this episode was quickly forgotten as our company shifted into crisis management mode. Within a few months, things between senior leadership and I smoothed over and our relationships healed. Both my manager and the leader of the Disney project even joined the panel of leaders who endorsed me for a promotion to executive director a year later. (To this day I believe my decisive action earned me a measure of respect in their eyes.)

In this extraordinary case, standing on my convictions was a matter of health—and potentially even life and death. In most other instances, the challenge of understanding when to stand on your convictions will be about how to drive positive business outcomes. This requires you to get comfortable in your skin and surroundings and recognize that your company hired you for a reason. You're there because of your talent and the value you bring. Standing up for what you believe in isn't always an easy thing to do, particularly as a Black person in corporate America. But to survive and thrive over the long term in this space, you've got to shed the burden of race and focus on doing what you do best.

For Black men in the corporate world, this is certainly a heavy demand—for all the reasons outlined in this book. But it is the key to unlocking your talent and providing it the air and space it needs to flourish. Standing on your convictions is a leap of faith that will carry your career to new heights if you know when and how to do it strategically.

Trust In The Talent, Skills, And Instincts That Have Carried You This Far

"I've lived a life that's full. I travelled each and every highway.
And more, much more than this—I did it my way."

—Frank Sinatra

"I'm telling you man, Georgetown gon' lose because John Thompson can't coach," Uncle Juan insisted. "Every time Georgetown has a big game, Thompson goes conservative and they lose. There is no way they are winning this game because John Thompson CAN'T COACH."

I was shocked to hear Uncle Juan say this about the venerable John Thompson—a coaching luminary who rose to fame while becoming a cultural force in the 1980s by turning the Georgetown Hoyas into a basketball powerhouse. (I used to think Georgetown was an HBCU[63] because of the all-Black men's basketball teams that Thompson boldly recruited to the school back then.)

The year was 1996 and Georgetown's electrifying team, led by Allen Iverson, was about to take on the mighty UMass Minutemen in the Elite 8 of the NCAA Tournament. I was visiting Uncle Juan's palatial McMansion in leafy West Windsor, New Jersey for the weekend. As I settled into the huge sectional couch in his living room, I rolled my eyes at his shocking words about the legendary Georgetown coach. "No freaking way, man," I shot back after he declared my boys would lose. "Georgetown's got this. UMass ain't got nothing for my man Iverson."

Like (virtually) every Black dude in America under the age of twenty-one back in 1996, I was 100% team Iverson during the 1996 NCAA Tournament. AI was a game-changing trendsetter on the

---

[63] Historically Black Colleges and Universities (HBCUs)

court with a wicked crossover dribble, crazy hops, and charisma. He just made it LOOK cool with his natural swagger draped in the vintage, kente cloth-patterned Georgetown unis (uniform) and Jordan 11s. All of us wanted to be Iverson back then, and there was no way in hell I thought they were gonna lose that game.

Sure enough, Uncle Juan was right. UMass did the unthinkable, shutting down Iverson while cruising to an easy 24-point win. After the game, Uncle Juan's criticisms of the late great John Thompson prompted me to take a second look at the coaching legend's record.

Despite recruiting and coaching legends like Iverson, Patrick Ewing, Dikembe Mutumbo, and Alonzo Mourning, Thompson's teams routinely dominated in the regular season before folding just about every year in the NCAA tournament.[64] Critics like my uncle blamed Thompson's habitual postseason failures on him not sticking with the approach that got his teams to the big games in the first place—and instead, going conservative in the most important moments. As I've advanced in my career, the example of John Thompson's teams falling short on the biggest stages has been instructive.

Whether you're a junior-level employee, mid-level manager, or a C-suite leader, your long-term success depends on your ability to trust in the approach that's earned you that seat at the table. Standing on your convictions is about more than just taking a stand for the things you believe in. It's also about trusting wholeheartedly in your ability and letting that inner confidence shine through in your work. Because if you don't trust your stuff, who will?

Calvin Butler, the CEO of Exelon—the largest utility company in the United States—echoes this point. While speaking on a panel at the 2024 Savoy Leadership Forum, Butler said that when Black

---

[64] Despite a stellar NCAA tournament record of 34-19, the Georgetown Hoyas only won one national title in John Thompson's 27 seasons.

leaders fail in the top jobs, it's because they stop doing the things that made them successful.

"The things that have gotten you there—people stop doing (when they get there,)" Butler told a roomful of senior Black corporate executives in April 2024. "They become risk averse, suddenly. My biggest piece of advice is—if you're going to fail at this job—fail doing it your way. I've gotten here doing it my way. Get good counsel but be yourself. Be authentic to who you are."

I wish Calvin Butler had been around to give me a pep talk during my tedious summer as an intern at Bloomberg News in 2004 because I was forced to learn this lesson the hard way. I'd landed that internship on the strength of being an enterprising reporter and editor for my campus newspaper. I was energetic, hungry, and aggressive—and thanks to my strong performance, readership for our little campus weekly soared to an all-time high during my tenure.

But then I got to Bloomberg, and like one of John Thompson's players in a big game, I transformed into the exact opposite of who I was on campus. I froze up, allowing myself to be intimidated by that newsroom, which is a fast-paced, market-moving machine. I also had the misfortune of landing on a news team led by a senior editor who wouldn't throw any assignments my way. I was one of two intern reporters on that team. The other intern—a young Asian American woman—was fed a steady diet of assignments, while I sunk into myself like a black hole—spending my days Googling, gorging on free junk food in Bloomberg's cafeteria, and watching the clock until it was time to get the hell out of there.

If I could go back in time, I'd give that younger version of myself an Mbappe-like kick in the pants and tell him to generate a few story ideas that would get the editor's attention. I was a young, would-be superstar who should have brought the same energy and approach to Bloomberg that I did in running my college paper. But unfortunately, I'd deviated from what got me to that point. I sat there, day after day, waiting for the editor to throw me a bone rather than taking the initiative on my own.

In fairness to that younger version of myself, I was reporting to a leader who had zero interest in helping me cultivate my talents. The few ideas I did pitch were quickly shot down, which was discouraging. But that's no excuse. I was given an opportunity on the big stage and lost my swagger. There was no Bloomberg job offer waiting for me after graduation, and I couldn't even blame them.

A Word On Letting Go

> "Sometimes letting go is a greater act of power than hanging on."
>
> —Eckhart Tolle, spiritual teacher

In August 2021, with the corporate world still loudly proclaiming a focus on diversity, equity, and inclusion initiatives, Shawn, a banking employee, landed a unique new assignment at a midwest based consumer bank where he'd worked for the past eight years. He was tapped by the CEO to launch a marketing strategy to help the firm improve the perception of its brand with Black Americans and grow its base of Black clients across all wealth and income levels. It was the type of role that suited the entrepreneurial-minded Shawn because it provided a chance to build something entirely new from the ground up.

For the effort's signature campaign, Shawn formed a partnership with a large media brand to create and execute a series of high-profile, community-facing events featuring fireside chats with celebrities, and interactive workshops to teach attendees strategies for growing wealth over the long term. The campaign, was wildly successful—with Shawn's efforts generating positive, high-profile media coverage for the bank. Shawn even succeeded in convincing several luminaries—including two current NFL legends to participate in his campaign. But best of all, the campaign brought in big dollars for the company—delivering a 550% profit over two years.

"I'd literally sketched this idea out with a pencil and paper in my kitchen one night, and to see it come to life, and even land some big names to participate was beyond anything I could have imagined," Shawn says. "It was fun to be a visionary, mobilize an entire bank around an effort, and then see it executed exactly as you'd envisioned it in your mind—right down to the last detail."

With such a staggering return on investment, Shawn expected to land a promotion and greater influence over the company's multicultural initiatives. "Instead," Shawn says, "they removed me from that project and assigned it to another executive, who was given global oversight of all multicultural marketing."

It wasn't all bad for Shawn, though, who received a sizeable bonus for his efforts, while still maintaining his remit as the head of marketing strategy for the Black segment. And while Shawn admits that having his signature project taken away for no good reason stings, he's accepted the change and maintains a big-picture perspective about what he's aiming to get out of his current position.

"Am I happy that this happened? Hell no. But at the end of the day, when you work for these corporations, you've got to accept that ultimately you don't own the work—they do," says Shawn, who's worked in the banking industry for the last 15 years. "This is their game board to play with and they can move the pieces around as they see fit."

Rather than putting up a fight over losing his signature project, Shawn remains focused on maintaining a strong performance in his current role, while leaning into creative ventures beyond his day job. "I'm actually glad it happened because it's given me that motivation to start plotting my next moves," he says. "If I didn't have anything else going on from a business standpoint beyond work, I'd be taking this a lot harder."

One of the most unpleasant aspects of corporate life is that you don't own the work that you produce. You can be tapped to build something new, lead with vision and conviction to make it happen, wildly succeed at it—and then be forced to watch as your project and role are handed over to another leader. I've gone through experiences like Shawn's and getting these little reminders you have no ownership over work that you poured your intellect and energy into hurts—and is a demotivator.

To maintain my mental (and spiritual) health in moments where I've lost an unwinnable battle—like what Shawn experienced—I fall back on the idea of non-attachment to any work I do on behalf of a corporation. This means not tying my happiness or sense of self-worth to my position in a company or any assignment I might be given from them. Within the corporate world, nothing is permanent. One moment, you can be riding high like Shawn was, and in the next—it can all be taken away in the blink of an eye. And on the flip side, although you may be going through a rough patch in your career—you can all but guarantee that good times will eventually come your way.

By maintaining a healthy non-attachment to your work, you'll reduce the suffering that comes when inevitable changes that aren't favorable land on your desk. It's okay—and healthy—to be proud of what you do and the position you worked so hard to earn. It's also okay to be passionate about your work and lead with conviction when you have good ideas that will benefit both your company's people—and its bottom line. Just take a mindful and balanced approach to your work—understanding it's impermanent and that there will be a time to let go of some aspect of it. Keeping a healthy distance through a level of non-attachment to your work will help you to remain content both when things are going your way and when they aren't.

CHAPTER SIX

ADAPT OR DIE—HOW TO SURVIVE AN EVER-CHANGING MARKETPLACE

"The measure of intelligence is the ability to change."

—Albert Einstein

Charles Darwin's theory of natural selection shines the spotlight on an uncomfortable truth about life on earth. It reveals that all creatures—from the microscopic to the massive—are locked in an everlasting struggle for survival. Darwin shows us that every living being on our planet is governed by a natural law that demands survival—all creatures must compete for resources within an ever-changing environment.

Those who adapt to Earth's continual changes don't merely survive, they thrive, multiply, and enjoy the spoils of our world for millennia. On the flip side, those who are unable to adapt are dealt a harsh set of cards that includes suffering, pain, death, and ultimately—extinction. The predator versus prey dynamic is a bedrock principle of this zero-sum competition. For one to win, the other must lose. Predatory species feed on others to survive—with the lives of (sentient) prey often ending in unimaginable terror, pain, and suffering. In other words—we live in a cold world where the name of the game is "kill or be killed."

Although capitalism is a human-made economic system, it bears striking parallels to Darwin's theory of natural selection. Competition is at the core of both systems. But instead of competing for natural resources like food and reproductive partners, companies duke it out for market share and profits. While nature rewards organisms that are best able to adapt to a changing environment, capitalism favors companies and people who successfully adjust to accommodate shifts in market demand and consumer tastes.

Meanwhile, beneath the fruits of the victorious of both nature and capitalism lie the remains of the less competitive. In nature, the species that fail to compete are chosen for extinction, while in capitalism, companies that fail to meet the demands of the ever-changing marketplace go the way of the dodo, woolly mammoth, and mastodon.[65] (The employees of these companies are collateral damage.) So, what does this mean for us as individual human beings who are living within this brutal economic system?

Today, we're experiencing a dramatic, tech-driven transformation in the way we live and work. We're living in a new world where our economy is increasingly rewarding the most adaptable people. The advent of new technologies like artificial intelligence ensures that we will see a full-scale revolution in our working lives in the coming decades, and against this backdrop, those of us who rely on a narrow skillset or area of expertise to make a living in the so-called "knowledge economy[66]"are at risk of becoming obsolete and "naturally selected" for removal from the marketplace. Conversely, those who

---

[65] The dodo, wooly mammoth and mastodon are all extinct creatures.
[66] The knowledge economy is a system of consumption and production based on intellectual capital.

embrace the adventure of lifelong learning while continuing to add to their skill sets will be best positioned to thrive over the long term.

This was a harsh lesson I was forced to quickly learn after graduating with a degree in journalism at the dawn of the Great Recession. I'd spent four years developing news reporting skills for an old media world that was suddenly coming to an end just as I was beginning my career. In what would become a running theme of my career—I'd have to adapt to become employable—and FAST.

A Lesson from the Black Mamba

"The wise adapt themselves to circumstances, as water molds itself to the pitcher."

—Chinese Proverb

Even though I am a diehard New York Knicks fan— which has been a painful existence for most of my four decades on this earth— I was a fan and admirer of Kobe Bryant throughout his time in the NBA and during his brief reinvention as an Oscar-winning filmmaker. Kobe was one of nature's chosen ones—a man blessed with otherworldly physical gifts, a sharp intellect, and an inner drive that pushed him to the top of his profession. As someone who was struggling to keep his head above water in corporate America, I drew inspiration from how Kobe continually adapted his game to stay a few steps ahead of his competitors in the NBA. In becoming an Oscar-winning filmmaker, Kobe also succeeded at something many athletes struggle with—adapting to a new identity when their playing days are over.

Kobe was a wing player during his twenty years in the league—a demanding role that required him to be both a leading scorer who took the most shots, as well as a defensive stopper who guarded the opposition's best player. What sets Kobe apart from most of his peers, historically, is how long he was able to dominate the NBA, even as the league drastically changed around him. When Kobe Bryant entered the NBA as a 17-year-old in 1996, the league played at a slower pace, with the rules and style of play favoring teams built around plodding big men, methodical offense, and butchering defense. Try watching a late 1990s-era Knicks-Heat or Bulls-Jazz postseason game on YouTube and you'll see what I mean. It's like watching grown men trying to run while underwater. Then compare that to the go-go era Phoenix Suns of 2005, or the Steph Curry Golden State Warriors of 2015.

In the decade before Kobe's retirement in 2016, the league began a rules-driven evolution towards a much faster pace and favored teams that could shoot well and play a more crowd-pleasing, free-flowing offensive style. Meanwhile, the starring role of the plodding big men, as well as the butchering defense, had been phased out of the game. The only way Kobe could last that long—and at such a high level of play—was to continually adapt and evolve along the way.

During the first phase of his career, Kobe was a ruthless scorer and hyperathletic dunker who relied on raw physical ability to drive to the basket at will. He drove his coaches and teammates crazy with how selfish and inefficient his style of play could be. But by the second phase of his career, with his explosiveness and athleticism declining, Kobe methodically worked to develop the best post-up and midrange scoring game in the entire league. Every summer, for nearly twenty years, Kobe added some new wrinkle to his repertoire to maintain his perch atop the NBA. He adjusted to his body's limitations over time and went from being a bouncy gazelle of an athlete to an uber-skilled all-around player with world-class footwork, the best mid-range skillset in the NBA and a post-up game that would give even Michael Jordan a run for his money.

In undergoing this continual metamorphosis, Kobe Bryant accomplished far more than simply extending his prime NBA years to their absolute limit. From afar, he provided corporate talent with an essential lesson on the importance of building on your core skills not just to survive a cold, Darwinian marketplace—but rather, thrive over the long term.

In the world of basketball, talented young men who expect to get by on raw athleticism without fully developing other aspects of their game never last long. Eventually, Father Time catches up with them as their youthful athleticism evaporates, and the league phases them out while they're still relatively young. The players who manage to hang onto their precious spots in the NBA through their late thirties are those who are most adaptable. Even as their athleticism dwindles, they find new ways of delivering production and value to their teams.

Although the career experience of an average corporate employee is vastly different from that of an NBA player, the same principle applies. The corporate employee who tries to get by as a one-trick pony without developing a broad range of transferrable skills doesn't just put themselves at risk of job elimination or obsolescence once reorgs or disruption lead to massive (and inevitable) change for their company or industry. They're also less marketable to prospective employers and unwittingly impose self-inflicted limitations on their long-term career prospects.

Recognize When It's Time To Move On

"My goal's to stay alive—survival of the fit, only the strong survive."

—Prodigy

The American Psychological Association defines adaptability as "the capacity to make appropriate responses to changed or changing situations." The Australian Psychological Society goes a step further and expands that definition to include "emotional regulation in response to change, novelty, variability, and uncertainty." In other words, you've got to master the ability to shift your approach when the situation calls for it and keep your cool in the process.

Without realizing it, I'd adopted this type of mindset early on in my career, and it's carried me to professional heights I couldn't have imagined. Today, I'm a banking industry executive[67], but growing up, I dreamed of becoming a sports columnist for either of New York's infamous tabloid newspapers—specifically the *Daily News* or *The New York Post*. I came of age reading the likes of local sports reporting legends like Mike Lupica, Vic Ziegel, Mark Kriegel, and Peter Vecsey—and was hell-bent on becoming their peer. Thanks to their work, I fell into the habit of reading the newspaper every day throughout middle school (sports section mostly) on the hour-long trek from Clinton Hill to Brooklyn's Dyker Heights Junior High.

Every morning, while the guys would spend their time on the B train flirting with and talking to girls, scrapping in the occasional fistfight, tagging the cars with graffiti, or doing death-defying stunts like riding between the cars or even "surfing[68]" the train—I'd be safely tucked away in the last car, nerding out alone with my copies of the Post and 'News. For a full hour, while *my peoples* got rowdy towards the front and middle of the train, I'd have that last car to myself, where I'd pore over box scores and read the latest tidbits about my Knicks, Yankees, Jets, and Giants.[69]

It was on those train rides that I fell in love with the idea of becoming one of the chosen few who got paid to attend sporting events and then write about 'em. I nurtured that dream throughout my four years of studying and practicing journalism in college. Unfortunately, it soon became clear after graduating that this would be a dream deferred. Darwinian market forces were killing off newspapers by the time I was ready to get into the game.

---

[67] As of this writing I work in banking, but that can always change!

[68] Subway surfing or sometimes called train surfing, is the act of riding on top or outside of a moving train.

[69] Yes, I do root for both NYC football teams. When they play each other, it's like watching two loved one's duke it out and I cease to have a rooting interest.

Tech behemoths like Google and Facebook were the new predators on the scene, and they were gobbling up all the ad revenues that newspapers once relied on to survive. Consumer tastes were also shifting for tech natives as an entire generation of young people never developed the habit of reading the paper every day but relying on their tech devices for instant news. The traditional industry had been too slow to realize it and lost to the emerging technology platforms. (I should have known better since I was the only kid in my entire class reading the newspaper on the subway!) Meanwhile, the advent of the smartphone was the final nail in the coffin for print media. The physical act of reading a print version of any news publication was slowly, dying off—but with the advent of the smartphone, slowly became precipitous, and the newspaper industry never figured out how to properly monetize this shift in consumer behavior. They also failed to find new ways to capture eyeballs in the budding attention economy.[70]

The wave of mass layoffs that decimated newspapers in 2008 accelerated in the coming decade and even a 'blind' person could see that a career as a newspaper reporter was no longer a viable option for a young upstart like me. With tens of thousands of dollars in student loan debt to repay, as well as the desire to do the basics like eat, pay rent, and build a life, I pivoted into one of the few areas where there was still strong demand for journalistic talent in a thoroughly disrupted industry: business reporting.

I nursed my Jones for sports journalism through blogging and regular appearances as a sports commentator on National Public Radio but writing market-moving stories about companies and financial markets is how I paid the bills and put food on the table. My two summer stints as a Bloomberg intern prepared me for this line of

---

[70] The term attention economy refers to the range of economic activities based on people's attention being treated as a scarce and highly desirable resource to be captured and maintained.

work and their archrival—Thomson Reuters—hired me as a stock market reporter during my last semester in college.

For nearly three years I grinded my way through that job before trying my hand in television as a production associate and reporter for ABC News. At the time I was still fixated on the world of sports and figured that by working at ABC—which shares the same parent company as ESPN—I'd be able to navigate my way into the world of full-time sports journalism. But in spite of my best efforts—which included pro bono freelancing along with endless, (fruitless) networking and job applications that went nowhere—it didn't happen, and after two years at ABC, I was completely burned out from the nerve-rattling world of high-stakes breaking news.

On a warm May afternoon in Spring 2010, I left ABC's corporate headquarters near Lincoln Center, never to return. In one of the saddest moments of my professional life, I turned my back on working full-time in mainstream media. Years of real-time deadlines, odd working hours, and sleeping with a Blackberry under my pillow left me exhausted both mentally and physically, and with a blood pressure that wasn't quite hypertensive—but still worrisome enough for me as a Black male who wasn't even thirty yet. Towards the end of my run at ABC, I realized I wasn't a fit for the network news lifestyle that came with an endless barrage of negative, soul-killing news, thwarted weekend plans, and zero room for mental health days. The news business had officially chewed me up and spat me out, and it was time to move on.

Future-Proof Your Career Through Skills Development

> "The future belongs to those who learn more skills and combine them in creative ways."
>
> —Robert Greene,
> author of "The 48 Laws of Power."

From my personal experience, every sports reporting job within the news industry may as well have been marked "need not apply." Between the lack of available jobs, the right connections to plug me in, and the industry's abysmal lack of diversity, I never stood a chance. Everywhere I turned, those doors were shut. Even today, the world of sports media remains largely closed to people of color and women. The sports journalists who cover your favorite teams are almost entirely white and predominantly male.[71] Beyond that, the entire industry was on shaky ground due to disruptive market forces, and the long-term earning potential in the profession was limited as well.

Given the tough hand I was dealt, I got over my disappointment and decided to get pragmatic. With at least a decade of student loans hanging over my head, I laid to rest my dream of becoming a featured columnist for my favorite publications (ESPN, Sports Illustrated, and my beloved New York tabloids) and set out on a mission to get PAID beyond the world of journalism with the skills I'd invested so much time in developing. But to do so, I'd have to first be able to articulate how my skills would bring value to an entirely different industry.

During my eight years as a reporter, I gained a decent amount of exposure to the inner workings of financial services companies and decided to focus on landing a job at a large firm with deep pockets and vast resources. I'd grown fascinated with the world of finance during my time at ABC, where I spent countless hours covering the Bernie Madoff scandal.[72] I also spent significant time writing for industry magazines about the origins of the global financial crisis and was enthralled by how the flow of capital impacted virtually

---

[71] ESPN – "Sports media remains overwhelmingly white and male, study finds." Sept. 22, 2021
[72] Bernie Madoff orchestrated the largest Ponzi scheme in U.S. history, defrauding investors out of an estimated $65 billion in a crime spanning nearly 20 years.

every aspect of our lives. And as an added plus, the industry paid well. Extremely well! (I wanted some of them bonus checks!)

My decision to pivot paid off—with dividends. It's carried me all the way to leadership roles at America's leading financial institutions. It's opened the door to me launching a successful real estate business. It's led to me gaining the ability to steer capital toward underserved communities and build and lead national programs aimed at closing the racial wealth gap. It also allowed me to collaborate with luminaries like Steph Curry, Kevin Hart, Condoleeza Rice, Keisha Lance Bottoms, Mellody Hobson—and others. I'm even a philanthropist now—and I invest money every year in causes that are near and dear to my heart.

The skills I'd spent so many years honing provided me with the ability to adapt when circumstances called for it. My time as a journalist sharpened my ability to write well and communicate clearly. Thanks to my experience covering the world of finance, I'd gotten pretty good at simplifying complex messaging for mass audiences and now could understand how to read a balance sheet. Since news reporters are often juggling numerous stories and beats simultaneously—all while nurturing relationships with trusted sources—I'd become a great project manager who could handle multiple high-profile initiatives at once.

As an added plus, I'd become immune to pressurized working environments. Once you've helped produce news programs on deadline for major TV networks where your work is seen by tens of millions of people or written stories that could move the entire stock market, you develop ice water in your veins. I knew I'd have no problem handling communications for a CEO, helping a company do damage control during a PR crisis, or building content marketing campaigns to entice consumers and advisors with financial services products.

The entire breadth of skills I'd developed opened a world of opportunity because they could be applied within any industry across a wide range of job levels. I may not have gotten a shot to do the work I'd dreamed about as a kid, but thanks to my wide arsenal of skills, the possibilities for my professional future were limitless.

Boost Your Adaptability Through Talent Stacking

"The idea of a talent stack is that you combine ordinary skills until you have enough of the right kind to be extraordinary."

—Scott Adams,
creator of the world-famous comic, Dilbert.

Back in the 1970s and 1980s—long before he became a globally syndicated cartoonist, TV show creator, best-selling author, and infamous right-wing media troll,[73] Scott Adams was your average, run-of-the-mill office worker bee. After studying economics in college, Adams took a job in corporate America, spending seven years at (the now defunct) Crocker National Bank where he worked as a teller (he was robbed at gunpoint twice,) budget analyst, and supervisor—among other jobs. From there, Adams spent nine years as a middle manager at Pacific Bell, while studying for a master's degree at night.[74]

To entertain himself during the endless boring meetings we all know and dread, Adams would doodle, and he'd draw cartoons of his bosses and colleagues. From these drawings emerged a character named Dilbert—a middle-aged engineer who hilariously toils through all the pain and ridiculousness of corporate life. For years, during his free time, Adams wrote comic strips about Dilbert's misadventures, and he'd pitch Dilbert to publications across the country. Newspapers and magazines turned Dilbert down left and right, but eventually, United Media took the bait.

---

[73] CNN – "Hundreds of newspapers drop 'Dilbert' comic strip after racist tirade from creator Scott Adams." Feb. 27, 2023
[74] Washington Technology – "Survival Guide Scott Adams, creator of "Dilbert" comic strip." Nov. 14, 2002

Together, Adams and United Media introduced the Dilbert comic strip to the world in 1989. Dilbert caught fire as white-collar workers everywhere identified with the strip—which featured characters any corporate employee can relate to, such as Catbert—the evil HR director, the incompetent Pointy-Haired Boss, and Wally, who is brilliant but has no ethical compass, and does the least amount of work required to not get fired.

Two years after its debut, Dilbert was syndicated in 100 newspapers across the country. Less than a decade later, Dilbert would be distributed to 2,000 news publications in fifty-seven countries and translated into nineteen languages. In 1999 it was even adapted into a TV show that aired for a couple of years.

But by 2013, Adams was venturing far beyond entertaining the corporate workers of the world through the eyes of Dilbert. For his next act, he introduced a concept that, when applied, can help talent everywhere maximize their long-term earning potential and adaptability in our corporate economy. Through a practice that he dubs "talent stacking," Adams says workers can make themselves more desirable to the marketplace by developing a variety of skills and then applying them in creative ways.

Here's how the concept works. As early as you possibly can, develop a singular in-demand skill that will serve as the foundation for the rest of your career. You don't even need to be a Kobe-level master of your chosen field. You just need to master about 95% of it. Next, you stack a few secondary skills on top of your foundational skills. The beauty of this next step is that you don't even need to be a full master in any of your secondary skills, either.

"Let's say you went to school to become an engineer. You would need to master about 95% of that field in order to be a good engineer at your job," Adams explains. "It's deceptively easy to pick up other layers, so long as you're only trying to pick up the important 80% … Imagine being an engineer who also understood business, could write well, knew how to speak in public, knew how to negotiate, and was a Master of Social Media. Well, even just good at social media. Well, then you're Elon Musk[75] because he has something like this—and an even bigger talent stack."

Your foundational skill is the area that you may have studied in school or spent years honing through apprenticeships or on-the-job training. The secondary skills are things you have a passing knowledge of and can become more proficient at through study and experience. In my case, my foundational skill is business writing, but I've managed to stack secondary skills on top of that due to my philosophy of only taking jobs that enable me to acquire new skills along the way.

For example, I once took a digital editor job at a large asset management firm even though it required me to provide leadership in areas where I had zero experience. The role put me in charge of search engine optimization (SEO) strategy for the entire firm and required me to ghostwrite for its fund managers and oversee the digital experience of its products from an editorial perspective. Thanks to diligent study and learning on the job, I'd mastered roughly 85% of each of these areas within my first six months and suddenly had a few hot new skills in fast-growing areas.

I flipped those skills into the most lucrative opportunity of my professional life up to that point when a bank approached me about leading external communications for a new line of business it was launching. I'd never officially worked in public relations. But my baseline skill of business writing, combined with my newfound ghostwriting and digital marketing "expertise" made me marketable enough to open the door to a career-elevating opportunity. Through studying, practice, and a few mistakes along the way, I mastered just enough of what I needed to succeed in that role as well.

My talent stack eventually led my career in an even more interesting and lucrative direction, and I picked up additional skills as a

---

[75] This is in no way an endorsement of Elon Musk, who in recent years has become a polarizing figure due to his stances and leadership on a wide range of issues.

marketer, corporate philanthropist, business manager, and public speaker.

Change is one of the few constants in our lives. Some changes—like the ones we see in nature— take place gradually, and over such long periods that you don't even notice them occurring. In other cases, such as life in corporate America, change comes at lightning speed, and often brings unpleasant circumstances like layoffs or reorgs that will shatter your world if you're not prepared to deal with them.

Through the power of talent stacking, you can increase your odds of being able to earn a nice living no matter what might be happening at any company you happen to be working for. Our future is uncertain. But it belongs to those who have the skills to navigate whatever circumstances it may bring their way.

Conclusion: 5 Tips To Improve Your Adaptability In The Professional World.

Stupid is the man who always remains the same.

- Voltaire

1. Never Stop Investing In Yourself

Father Time is undefeatable, but LeBron James is giving him a run for his money. Long after all his peers from the NBA's iconic 2003 draft class retired and were well into their second acts in life, LeBron remained a dominant force in the league at age 40—and counting. He's only the sixth player to make it to the 21st season in the NBA, but unlike most of those players, LeBron's level of play didn't fall off one bit as he advanced in age. So, what's his secret? According to The Ringer's Bill Simmons, LeBron invests HEAVILY in his body. In a 2016 episode of The Ringer podcast,[76] Simmons recalls a conversation

---

[76] The Ringer, June 8, 2016

he had with LeBron's lifelong friend and business manager, Maverick Carter. According to Simmons, Carter revealed that LeBron spends more than $1.5 million a year to keep his body at peak physical condition. This includes employing the best chefs, masseuses, and trainers that money can buy. Carter also told Simmons that LeBron installed the very same gym equipment that his Miami Heat and Cleveland Cavaliers teams used at their facilities at his home. LeBron designed every aspect of his life to help him achieve optimal health and maximize his performance on the basketball court.

There's an important lesson for corporate talent in the approach that LeBron takes towards his career. He invests HEAVILY in himself so that he can stay on top. No matter what your background may be, recognize that investing in YOURSELF is the best investment YOU WILL EVER MAKE. Investing in yourself means devoting your time, energy, and money towards becoming the best version of yourself possible. There are all sorts of ways to invest in yourself. It includes the physical, which involves getting routine medical and dental checkups, eating right, and going to the gym. On the financial side, it could mean developing your side hustle into a full-fledged business or working with an advisor to get your finances in order. Investing time and energy towards causes and relationships that matter to you will help you create meaning and purpose in your life. And when you add up all the returns on these investments in yourself, it'll result in a life well lived. As a bonus, your return on investment will include a career that stands the test of time—just like LeBron.

2. **Embrace Lifelong Learning**

One of the saddest aspects of our way of life is that we spend roughly our first two decades bubble-wrapped in environments that encourage learning, only to eventually be thrust into a cold, Darwinian marketplace that reduces our lives to a focus on earning enough money to survive until the day we die. Suddenly, the world of endless wonder and possibility that we experienced in our youth shrinks to whatever responsibilities we have at work—along with the permanent grind of keeping a roof over our heads, clothes on our backs, and food in the fridge. Now look, each of these areas is important in its own way but they do not stop us from expanding, even long after we've taken that last academic course, and shifting into self-driven learning. Continuous learning will enrich and help you discover talents you didn't even know you had. It will give you a deeper understanding of the world around you and help you build new relationships. It will help you keep up with the latest technology. It will help you deliver more value on the job, and beyond that—lifelong learning will help you become resilient in the face of the inevitable uncertainties and setbacks you'll face in every aspect of your life. Lifelong learning will help you futureproof your life.

3. Harness Your Brain's Superpower For Adaptability

They say you can't teach an old dog new tricks. Fortunately, this doesn't apply to humans. In fact, our brains are wired for learning and adaptability, according to the Stanford neuroscientist and podcaster Andrew Huberman. According to Huberman, our brains possess something called neuroplasticity—which is the brain's ability to change and adapt in response to stimuli over time. Even as fully grown adults, our brains can build new connections between neurons and neural networks in a process called neurogenesis. So, what does this mean? Huberman says it means that contrary to popular belief, brain development doesn't just happen in childhood.

Our brains are still capable of growth, even as adults. The catch is we must be active participants in the continued development of our brains. Think of your brain as a muscle that can be worked out just like your abs and pecs.

The beauty of all this is that even though we live in a harsh, uncertain world, we can wire our brains for continued learning which will increase our abilities to adapt to any situation the world may throw our way. Scientists point to several techniques that can be leveraged to boost the neuroplasticity of our brains, including eating the right foods, getting proper rest, and engaging in mind-bending activities such as playing chess, learning new words regularly and even training ourselves to use our non-dominant hand for everyday activities like brushing our teeth.

> "It can help to think of your brain in terms of a muscle," says Dr. Lynda Shaw, a chartered psychologist and cognitive neuroscientist who is a Fellow of The Royal Society of Medicine and an Associate Fellow of the British Psychological Society. "If you do enough bicep curls you'll increase the size of your biceps. It's the same process with your brain. If you exercise your brain correctly and often, neuroplasticity means it will become more powerful.[77]"

4. Don't Limit Yourself To Professional Labels Or Titles

The late, great Virgil Abloh is best known for his barrier-busting approach to the worlds of fashion and design. Before his untimely death from a rare cancer in 2021, Abloh was one of the most powerful Black executives in the corporate world, and his artistry earned him comparisons to the likes of Andy

---

[77] Source: Atlassian - 9 neuroplasticity exercises to boost productivity. Feb. 9, 2022

Warhol and Jeffrey Coons, as well as a level of fame that's uncommon for a fashion designer. But one of the most interesting things about Abloh is he didn't go to school to study fashion or the arts in a conventional sense. By trade, he was an architect, and he'd studied civil engineering when he was in college. Yet Abloh never boxed himself into the labels of fashion designer, architect, or engineer. Instead, he described himself as a "maker," and in addition to fashion, he designed everything from clothing and Kanye West album covers, to Evian water bottles, Big Mac containers for McDonald's, a rug for Ikea—and many other corporate collaborations.

So, what's the lesson in all this? Take a page from Abloh and don't limit your identity or perception of yourself to whatever your job happens to be at a particular moment. Who you are is not tied to whatever company you happen to work for. You don't have to box yourself into earning a living in whatever subject you majored in during your college or grad school days. These titles and money can be snatched away at a moment's notice. And when that happens, what are you left with? As Jay-Z says:[78] "When you're tight—and you say, 'I only do this,' you constrict yourself. So, nothing can come in."

Maintain an open mind about your professional identity and be open to new possibilities for how you can apply your skillsets in our ever-changing marketplace.

5. Be Like Kobe! Commit To Picking Up New Skills

I once had a cool manager who got laid off at the ripe old age of 59. He didn't have enough money to retire. He had two daughters who were in college and an expensive mortgage

---

[78] Source: Boom Bap Nation – "Rakim Gives JAY-Z His Flowers For Quoting 'I Know You Got Soul' Classic."

for a gorgeous house in Connecticut. Beyond that, his very identity was tied up in his long-time role at the financial services firm we worked for. He loved that job and coasted in it for fifteen years without investing in himself to develop new skills or even sharpen his existing ones. Finding that next opportunity at his age didn't come easy since our marketplace is unkind to older white-collar workers like him. Eventually, he was forced to start dipping into his retirement savings earlier than he expected to. Nearly five years would pass before he'd find another opportunity at a more junior level.

So, what's the moral of this depressing tale? If you're in corporate America long enough, you'll be blessed to find a few rare moments where you're coasting along in your job. You're good at it and you can function like you're on autopilot. It's during times like these that you should seize the moment to invest in yourself. Maybe there's an advanced degree that you've had your eye on or a new certification you've been thinking about. Or perhaps you can finally build out your side hustle. Whatever it is, be sure to challenge yourself to build your knowledge base or skillset. And when circumstances inevitably force you to adapt, you'll be ready to meet the challenge head-on.

CHAPTER SEVEN

THE SECRETS TO NETWORKING THE RIGHT WAY

"The way of the world is meeting people through other people."

—Robert Kerrigan, author

In December 2005, New York City came to a standstill at the height of the holiday shopping season because of a transit strike. The city was mired in a bitter early-winter cold snap, and in those days before Uber and Lyft, it was damn near impossible to get anywhere on time with NYC's buses and subways out of commission.

As a result, I was an hour late for my final round interview with one of the largest news outlets in the world, Thomson Reuters—which would be my first job fresh out of college. That final interview—which I was fortunately able to push back at the last minute— would turn out to be unlike any job interview I've ever experienced.

After surviving the initial HR screening, a writing test, and separate interviews with several senior editors, I was brought in for a final meeting with a handful more senior editors—not a single person of color among them—for a grilling that felt more like a high-stakes press conference or testimony before Congress. This wasn't a scenario I was mentally prepared for, and it caught me completely off guard.

"You're an hour late. Minus two points for you," one of the editors joked when I entered the room.

The intimidating setting inflamed my normal job interview jitters, and my inexperience was on full display as the panel lobbed question after question at me. These questions weren't softballs either. In stark contrast to previous interviews that were conversational, these questions were more like hand grenades that required me to think quickly on my feet in front of an audience. I stammered my way through as best I could while my heart rate surged, as sweat beaded my forehead and moistened the palms of my hands and armpits.

I had a lot riding on this. Launching my journalism career at Thomson Reuters wouldn't just put my entry-level pay on the high end of what a freshly minted college graduate could expect to earn as a journalist. Landing this job would stamp my credentials in the corporate world and serve as the foundation for a career that could take me wherever I wanted. In those days before the media industry was decimated by declining revenues and mass layoffs, journalists spent years preparing for a chance to work in a shop like Thomson Reuters. And here I was, some kid fresh out of leading a campus newspaper with a chance to maybe skip to the front of the line and start my career at a prime outlet.

Even getting to this point was a major achievement. And I owed it all to sage advice I'd received from Dr. Ralph Engelman, an old college professor who recommended I join the National Association of Black Journalists (NABJ) at the end of my sophomore year. Joining NABJ proved to be one of the best professional decisions I'd ever made. It was one of those life-altering decisions you don't realize is so pivotal when you're in the heat of the moment.

Which brings us to the first secret to networking the right way.

Secret #1: Join A Black Professional Network

"I don't see anywhere on your resume that you're Black," Dr. Ralph Engelman said in a calm, professorial tone, as he pored over my bare-bones CV. This was the pre-LinkedIn era when recruiters couldn't just look you up online. Engelman took office hours with college upperclassmen to help them strategize on the next steps for their careers. And for the most promising students, Dr. Engelman would sometimes even leverage his connections to help them land jobs and internships. "Let's get you a student membership in the National Association of Black Journalists," he said.

Without saying so explicitly, Dr. Engelman—a White man—was teaching me to view my race as an asset that could help me get my foot in the door at one of the nation's leading news outlets. Diversity was, and continues to be, a deep-rooted problem in newsrooms and corporations across America. So, if you happen to be a person of color with enough talent and charisma to get the job done, you're a unicorn in a sense. And whether you're in the news business or another field, corporate America is on the lookout for people like you. I absorbed Dr. Engelman's view that companies are in desperate need of talented people from diverse backgrounds who can step right in and get the job done.

Thanks to Dr. Engelman's advice, I applied for NABJ's student internship program for rising juniors and seniors, which served as a feeder of prospective Black talent to mainstream news outlets. This paved the way for me to land an internship at Bloomberg News, where I'd spend the next two summers working on their news desk. As my Bloomberg stint ended, NABJ hosted a job fair during their annual convention, where I had a fateful encounter with recruiters from Thomson Reuters.

A Black professional network provided me with a strong foundation for my career. Through the years, I've found these networks vital in building contacts who aren't just a source of career opportunities but serve as guides on how to navigate companies and industry, as well as a source of information exchange that helped me stay up to date on the latest developments in my industry.

In my case, NABJ set me up for a great entry-level opportunity coming out of college. I just had to survive the Reuters interview gauntlet first. And unfortunately for me, I came dangerously close to blowing the biggest opportunity of my professional life to that point.

Secret #2 Avoid Isolation At All Costs

"We don't function well as human beings when we're in isolation."

—Robert Zemeckis, filmmaker

My interview for an entry-level reporting role at Reuters was by far, the worst job interview of my entire career. It was awful. I was a wide-eyed, inexperienced guppy who was trying to swim with sharks, and it showed. But fortunately, luck was with me on this go around. Sensing me flailing, one of the editors on the panel—a British dude named Eddie who I'll never forget, threw me a much-needed lifeline.

As the room sat in awkward silence for a moment that seemed to last an eternity, Eddie blurted out: "Well, Justin DID show himself to be a pretty good writer on our test. I think he did just fine there."

When the interview finally ended, I left the Reuters headquarters, dejected, knowing deep down this was an opportunity lost. As I began a brisk walk to Penn Station in the frigid, late-December air, Marty[79], the editor-in-charge, called my cell phone.

"There's a bit of skepticism about you, but we're going to give you a chance," he said through a thick UK accent. "We want to see what you can do over the next three months before we make a final decision."

---

[79] This is a pseudonym to protect the person's identity.

This meant I'd have roughly 12 weeks to prove I had the chops to make it as a stock market reporter, or otherwise be sent packing.

My Dad was the first person I called (to share my "kinda sorta" good news.)

"I'm proud of you, son," he said. Although we were separated by thousands of miles, I could hear the smile in his voice. But despite winning my father's praise, I was hardly inspired or filled with confidence as I began to mentally prepare for the journey ahead. And over the next three weeks, as my first day approached, my mind kept replaying Marty's smug remark on a loop: "There's a bit of skepticism about you."

I envisioned the editors in that room debating, "Nah, we can't hire that guy. No way. He's not cut out for this place."

And then Eddie argues his case: "But clearly the test shows he has some talent. It's not an easy test and it's obvious that he's capable of doing the work."

Marty's candidness about their skepticism sent me down a rabbit hole of self-doubt. And rather than feeling excitement about starting my first job, I was instead gripped by fear.

- Fear that I was being allowed into a place where I truly didn't belong.
- Fear that I wasn't good enough for the opportunity that was being handed to me on a silver platter.
- Fear that I was an imposter.
- Fear that my Black face had no place within that predominantly White space.
- Fear that some diversity initiative was the only reason I was even being given a shot in the first place. (I owed the opportunity to NABJ, after all.)

Most of all, I feared their skepticism of me was justified.

At the most formative moment of my career, fear put a death grip on my psyche. And nearly a decade would pass before I grew confident enough in my abilities to shake off the fear that Marty's words struck within me.

I was afraid to step into the Reuters newsroom on my first day. And as a result, fear would ultimately doom my tenure before it even began. That fear would put me into a psychological shell that I'd struggle to come out of for my entire time at Thomson Reuters.

But on the plus side, at least I didn't have to wonder where I stood with these people. It was crystal clear that from day one, I wasn't seen by my superiors as a talented, high-potential cub reporter. I wasn't the hotshot first-round draft pick who'd be joining the team to much acclaim. Instead, I was more like that undrafted free agent—the overlooked scrub who displays just enough raw talent to be given a shot to compete for a spot on the team coming out of training camp.[80]

My survival instincts shifted into overdrive during that three-month probation. I nailed every assignment they threw my way, pitched and wrote as many stories as I could, and even took up some secretarial duties—answering phones for the Americas news desk. I was determined not to give these people a reason to send me packing.

But those three months were hardly a walk in the park. Within that bustling, high-energy newsroom, I was an island to myself. Entirely isolated, day after day I ate lunch alone. I took coffee breaks alone. It felt like I could go days on end without interacting with anyone in the newsroom beyond the occasional conversation with an editor about a story I was working on. And while all around me reporters worked together within the rhythm of the newsroom, eating together at lunches, gossiping at the water cooler, and hanging out at happy hours—I ground it out on my own for those three months.

---

[80] In the NBA, for example, first round draft picks are guaranteed spots on the team, while second round picks enjoy a strong change of making it. Undrafted free agents have to truly stand out to earn a spot on the team.

The racial makeup of that newsroom compounded the feeling of isolation. Although there were a handful of Black people working there—three of whom were reporters, with two working as clerical employees—it was a predominantly White space with zero Black people in senior-level editorial roles and just two women of color in leadership positions.

Nevertheless, I shifted my social unease to the back of my mind and instead focused on what I could control—which was the quality of work I put in. I made sure anything I touched was solid. And my efforts paid off. After the three months were up, I'd done enough to surpass their low expectations and landed the job full-time when my probation was lifted.

But I was still an island in that newsroom. It was like being in middle school without anyone to sit with at lunchtime. I needed someone who could help me plug into the social rhythms of the place. You can't do your best work if you're not comfortable. And if you're not comfortable in your workplace, you're not going to last long.

Which brings us to secret number three.

Secret #3 Cultivate a mentor (or two)

> "A mentor is someone who can give you guidance, advice, and support when you need it."
>
> —Richard Branson,
> co-founder, of The Virgin Group

Onboarding is one of the most vulnerable stages of the employer-employee relationship. This is the three-month period where employees are officially introduced to their new colleagues and workspaces, while finally getting a hands-on understanding of their roles and responsibilities. Onboarding is an extension of the interview process in a sense. This means that virtually every task, no matter how great or small, is being judged by superiors and colleagues alike. As you're settling into the job, they're sizing you up.

For talent, the first three months is a time to absorb the unwritten rules of the new company, assimilate into the corporate culture, and get a firm grasp of what's expected over the near and long term.

Smart companies use the onboarding period to make new joiners feel a sense of belonging. They provide their employees with psychological safety, which frees them up to do the jobs they were hired to do at the highest level they're capable of. Companies use onboarding to train employees on how to execute their jobs while educating them on key policies and procedures.

When companies get the onboarding process wrong, it can lead to turnover. In fact, 30% of employees quit after ninety days for a variety of reasons, including bad experiences, problems fitting into the corporate culture, and poor leadership [81]—all of which can be traced back to onboarding.

My Reuters superiors had no idea how close I came to being one of the 30% who called it quits after ninety days. (The only reason I didn't give up, was because I had no clue at the time what else I could do to pay back my student loans. Additionally, I feared quitting too soon would damage my long-term career prospects. I was determined to survive there for a year, maybe even two.)

The first error on the company's part was that instead of an onboarding process during my Reuters stint, I was given probation. Once that probation was up, there was no warm welcome into the fold—no sense of belonging. No psychological safety. Leadership had made it clear they were skeptical of me as a fit so I came to work every day with eyes in the back of my head. Anxiety was my companion. I was suddenly swimming in the deep end of the pool with no lifejacket and an implicit order that it was time to sink or swim.

The misery of my first three months eventually extended into six, and I was struggling to find a groove. But just when I was near my absolute breaking point, I caught a break in the form of a challenging assignment

---

[81] Source: 2022 Job Seeker Nation Report

that would force me to come out of my shell and connect with someone—ANYONE, in that newsroom who could show me the ropes.

My new assignment was to write a weekly column about initial public offerings (IPOs). IPOs enable companies to raise capital and occur when a privately owned company sells stock to the public for the first time on an exchange. Shares of big-name companies that are going public for the first time typically help their leaders raise billions as investors trip over themselves to get a piece of the action.

At the time of my assignment, I had no idea what an IPO was, but I was determined to become an expert overnight! I needed to understand which IPOs were worth writing about, how to spot trends in the marketplace that would impact new offerings, and how to build expert contacts within that space who would serve as sources for my stories. It was a daunting assignment, and I knew I needed a guiding hand to look over my shoulder if I was going to succeed.

So, in addition to studying a full year's worth of stories in the Reuters file—plus all the industry analysis I could get my hands on—I went out of my way to build a relationship with Sam,[82] a more seasoned reporter who'd held the IPO beat before me. As luck would have it, Sam was a chill dude. He was a bookish cat from Boston with an easygoing, yet professorial demeanor. For my first few weeks on the beat, Sam gave me a heads-up on key IPOs that were worth reporting on and plugged me in with industry contacts whose insights would help me generate compelling story ideas. He even let me run the first drafts of my stories past him before I filed them with the copy desk.

Sam and I never became friends, and we didn't need to either. But as a newsroom veteran, Sam seemed to appreciate having a newbie reach out to him for advice and direction on how to navigate a beat. Beyond having a veteran whose brain, I could pick—I appreciated, FINALLY, having some type of regular human connection in the office. Suddenly, I wasn't an island anymore.

---

[82] This is a pseudonym to protect the person's identity.

Sam and I settled into a routine for a couple of months, where I'd run story ideas past him and let him review my copy to ensure I had all the nuances right. Eventually, I developed enough confidence and experience that I no longer needed the same type of hands-on guidance. Thanks to Sam's mentorship, I survived my initial growing pains in that newsroom.

But it was on me to cultivate Sam as a mentor. As the mentee, it was also incumbent on me to be respectful of my mentor's time and busy schedule and come prepared with the specific areas I needed guidance.

Over the years since, as I've progressed in my career and reached the executive ranks, the need for a mentor has never fully gone away. There are always daunting new goals to strive for as well as difficult challenges to navigate, and a trusted advisor (or two) can be an awesome resource to turn to for advice.

The common thread in mentor-mentee relationships, regardless of the level you have attained in your company, is that as the mentee, you are the one who drives the direction of the relationship. I always look to cultivate relationships with amiable people who have integrity and expertise in an area I need to learn about. After making those connections, I'm specific about the guidance I need, and I bring structure to the relationship by reporting on the progress I've made toward achieving my goals. Once those goals are achieved, the relationship should evolve. It's perfectly okay for mentors to come and go but always keep an eye out for the next one who can guide you to the next level. As you grow in your life and career, that's how it should be.

Secret #4 - Get Yourself an Office Bestie (or three)

> *"Sometimes you want to go where everybody knows your name, and they're always glad you came."*
>
> —Lyrics from "People Like Us," the theme song to the 1980s hit show, "Cheers."

Despite a rocky start to my Thomson Reuters career, I'm proud of the work I did there. I delivered market-moving journalism in that newsroom that I'll remember till the day I stop working. But the sad reality is, that I never felt like I belonged at Reuters. Between the skepticism I was greeted with from day one by the senior leadership team, and my failure to connect with colleagues on an organic level, it was a minor miracle I lasted there for two years.

Leaving Reuter's for the final time felt like a weight was being lifted off my chest. Thank goodness, every job I've held since has felt easy by comparison. My Reuters experience is one that many Black people throughout corporate America can relate to. Using my Reuters experience as an example, I suspect that many Black people are eyeing the exits because of difficulty in finding their tribe within the company. Indeed, research shows that more than one in three Black employees intend to leave their current jobs within the next two years and that they're thirty percent more likely to leave their jobs than White employees are.[83] Missing a sense of belonging is a big reason why. This can be traced back to a lack of diverse representation both in the executive and employee ranks throughout America's largest, most influential companies.

Looking back on my career, the jobs I've enjoyed the most were those where I developed strong bonds with the people I worked with and for. At these companies, I was able to break through perceived social barriers and develop friendships that transcended race and gender even if forged within the fire of the work. Not coincidentally, I've stayed the longest at companies where my relationships were the strongest.

So, how do you go about building friendships at work? There's no secret sauce but the one thing you must do is get out of your head and take the initiative. To make a friend, you've got to first BE a friend. Try grabbing lunch with a colleague you seem to have a strong rapport with, regardless of what their racial or gender background

---

[83] Source: Coqual – Being Black in Corporate America – An Intersectional Exploration

might be. Use that time to find what you may have in common with that person outside of work and then build your relationship from there. Do this a few times a month with a variety of colleagues. Mix in some coffee and happy hours, too, while you're at it.

During my tenure working for a large asset management firm, I went several steps beyond mere lunches, coffees, and happy hours, and wound up making some of the best friends of my adult life. I invited a couple of colleagues to join a softball team I created, the BK Broilers. God, that team was awful. In its two years of existence, the BK Broilers never won a single game! But thanks to the shared experience of laughing over beers at how awful that team was, I became close friends with two White colleagues on the team, along with an industry contact who also became a good friend. We keep in touch on a group chat to this day, and we've even gone on a couple of fellas' trips over long holiday weekends. I had some of the most fun times of my career with people I'd developed legitimate friendships with while working.

Beyond performance, friendships are a key to your long-term success at whatever company you happen to work for. Research supports this view. According to Gallup[84], employees who have a best friend at work are significantly more likely to succeed at:

- Engaging customers and internal partners
- Accomplishing more in less time
- Innovating and sharing ideas
- Having fun while at work

Work friends will help elevate your performance. But on the flip side, research shows that the loneliest employees deliver the worst performance.[85] So, do yourself a favor and make some besties.

---

[84] Source: Gallup - "The increasing importance of a best friend at work." Aug. 17, 2022
[85] Source: Academy of Management Journal – "
No employee an island: Workplace loneliness and job performance." 2018

Secret #5 -Prioritize Learning And Discovery In Your Networking

"Your network is your net worth."

—Porter Gale, author

Despite my difficulties fitting in at Reuters, I'll always cherish the place for one of the most crucial disciplines it trained me to build in my career: networking. The best reporters are constantly working to cultivate a network of sources who will give them the intel that makes for the best news stories. And, as a reporter, you can't build a network of sources without working the phone and getting off your tush to hold face-to-face meetings over lunch, coffee, or drinks with people who are in the know. (In a hybrid environment, Zoom meetings are another approach. Just beware of Zoom fatigue.)

For a news reporter, there's an obvious transactional element to networking. You can build a whole career as a reporter off just a handful of reliable, trusted sources. After moving onto an entirely different line of work and serving in large companies with tens of thousands of people, I've kept up that habit of cultivating a network of reliable sources, and it's served me well. Only this time, I'm not doing it to generate fodder for stories that can move the stock market, I'm doing it to learn. I want to be an expert in both my industry and company. I want to bounce big ideas off people of influence within the company who can help me refine those ideas into projects I can bring to life. I want to know what's happening in other departments or lines of business. I want to become friends with the people who are in the know. Internally, I want the type of information that can help me stay informed about the health and future of the company so I can make informed decisions about my future. I can't get that information by just putting my head down and focusing solely on my immediate role and responsibilities.

For introverts, networking can be stressful. Regardless of your personality type, if you prioritize networking as a means for learning and discovery, you won't only get access to vital information or ideas that will help you make informed decisions about your career. You may also be slowly positioning yourself for a climb up the corporate ladder.

On multiple occasions in my career, my approach to networking helped me to turn big ideas I'd been developing into stretch assignments that boosted my profile and helped me to grow my influence in the company despite being of lower rank on the org chart. Even as a junior or mid-level employee, you can build enough influence to move an entire bureaucracy if you've got friends in the right places along with intel to help you manifest your ideas.

So, get out there and network. (With learning and discovery as the focus of your conversations.)

Secret #6 - Get Yourself an Executive Sponsor

Mentors are important. They're there to serve as guides who can provide moral support and career coaching, especially around specific challenges. But to really get ahead in any corporation, you need an executive sponsor.

In most instances, your executive sponsor won't be the person you report to. An executive sponsor is a senior leader within your company (or department) who will use their clout to help you advance your career. This is the person who will be your advocate in the room when leadership is deciding who should be promoted or get a chance to lead a high-profile initiative.

Landing an executive sponsor is far easier said than done though, especially if you're Black. According to Harvard Business Review (HBR) while only 20% of White employees have an executive sponsor—just 5% of Black employees have one.

For Black people, sponsorship can have a transformative impact on a career. Research shows that a Black manager is 65% more likely to reach the next rung on the corporate ladder if they have an executive sponsor.[86] They're also 60% less likely to quit their jobs if they have one.[87]

I can attest to this personally because I've had several executive sponsors in my career, and each time these relationships led the way to plum assignments, promotions, pay increases, and fatter bonus checks. But how do you go about finding an executive sponsor?

The unfortunate reality for Black talent is there's no simple answer to this question. Black senior leadership in corporate America continues to be scarce[88] and research shows that the fortunate few who ascend to these heights are reluctant to sponsor Black talent over fears of how it may be perceived.[89] So, odds are you'll need a White senior leader as your sponsor.

And that's okay because I've had several in my career. Here are some tips for landing an executive sponsor:

1. **You've Got To Be A Superstar**

    This is an obvious one, but for starters, you've got to be a superstar in your job to even get on the radar of senior leadership in the first place. And then once you're on their radar, they'll want to put their political muscle behind a protégé whose performance is going to make them look good in the long run. The sponsor-beneficiary relationship is a two-way street. While they can absolutely help turbocharge your career, you'll boost their careers as well. HBR notes that managers and executives who proactively sponsor talent are

---

[86] Harvard Business Review: "20% of White Employees Have Sponsors. Only 5% of Black Employees Do." Feb. 10, 2022

[87] Harvard Business Review: "20% of White Employees Have Sponsors. Only 5% of Black Employees Do." Feb. 10, 2022

[88] Source: McKinsey Research: "In corporate America, Black senior leadership remains scarce." March 11, 2021

[89] Harvard Business Review: "20% of White Employees Have Sponsors. Only 5% of Black Employees Do." Feb. 10, 2022

more likely to climb the ladder themselves. Their careers can also stall out if they bet on the wrong horse. So don't be that dud horse.

2. **Land Yourself In A Role That Can Get You Access To Senior Leaders**

The one common denominator for me each time I landed an executive sponsor was that I held a mid-level role that provided me with access to senior leadership regularly. This gave them ample opportunity to see my great work. And I used their feedback on my work as a launch point for relationship building. I did this the same way I went about making friends in the office: through asking for invitations to coffee or lunch, or even regular old meetings. With some leaders, this led to relationships that evolved into formal sponsorship. In other cases, there was no chemistry and I moved on.

The data certainly tells a discouraging story for Black people about the challenge of finding an executive sponsor. But it's not impossible. Navigating your way into a position that will get you visibility with leadership is a key tactic to deploy.

3. **Play The Long Game**

Even after you identify an executive who has the political capital to open doors for you, it'll take time to build relationship equity with them. Your senior leadership relationships won't evolve into formal sponsorship overnight. They need time to size you up and see your potential. They need to learn more about how you're perceived by peers and leaders throughout the organization. You also need to size them up as well. Is this leader a person of integrity that you can trust? In every case where I landed an executive sponsor, it took me more than a year (and on one occasion two years) at the company to land one, so buckle up and patiently play the long game.

4. Don't Be Afraid To Ask

Once you've established a reservoir of trust and relationship equity with a senior leader, making the ask is the next step. Just be clear about what it is you're looking for when you make that ask. Explain to them what you're trying to accomplish and how their support can help you get there. Volunteer to take on stretch assignments they can plug you into. Have them connect you to other senior leaders as well. And then establish a regular cadence of touchpoints with them. (If they agree to sponsor you, get on their calendar as soon as possible.)

The worst thing that can happen is the senior leader tells you they can't do it. And even if they turn down the chance to be your sponsor, they'll still be flattered by the offer, and you'll gain another friend in a high place.

Secret #7 - Add Some Mentees To Your Network

If you're doing enough of the right things in your life and career, you're going to be seen by up-and-comers as someone to emulate. One of the greatest signals that you're more successful than you might think is suddenly younger people and less experienced colleagues are hitting you up for advice. If you're fortunate enough to have this happen to you, lean into it.

You don't even need to be a senior leader in your firm to serve as a mentor. Back in my entry-level Reuters days, I served as a mentor to both college journalists and high school students.

Becoming a mentor is a great way to grow as a leader. It places you into a role where you're guiding someone else, and as you gain experience in doing this, you'll start to build confidence in your ability to influence and inspire others. This makes mentoring a great training ground to prepare for the next level in your career.

But as a mentor, require your mentee to value the time you're giving them. Challenge them to provide a focus for your meetings with specific areas they need guidance in. And remind them that ultimately, their growth is about the work they're willing to put in. You're there as a trusted advisor, but it'll be on them to act on the insights you've imparted.

As a mentor, it's also important to remember you've got two ears and one mouth. To be an effective mentor, you need to be an active listener who has genuine empathy for the person you're guiding. The best corporate leaders are masters at active listening and empathy. On a human level, serving as a mentor is one of the most deeply satisfying things you can ever do in your career.

Secret #8 -Prioritize Your LinkedIn Presence (But Don't Overdo It)

There's a rock-star CEO who leads a Fortune 500 company that I know personally and absolutely adore. But I had to mute this person's LinkedIn posts. It felt like every other day they were out there oversharing about their life and career.

If you work in corporate America, there's an unwritten rule that you must have a presence on LinkedIn. Think of LinkedIn as your professional highlight reel. It's a place to showcase your talents and accomplishments and to connect with folks throughout your industry and area of expertise. But there's a right way to use it. Here are a few tips:

1. **Invest In A Professionalized Profile Picture**

    Your profile picture is an advertisement of yourself to the world. You want the highest quality photo possible here and you need to look your absolute best. Leave that to professionals who can help. You'll reap dividends in your career off the modest investment in a professional-grade profile picture. (A great background photo is a nice finishing flourish as well.)

2. **Leverage Artificial Intelligence To Optimize Your Profile**

   When recruiters and users are searching for people or content on LinkedIn, they use keywords to find what they're looking for. You'll want to make sure your profile is reeling in the types of users you want to connect with, and AI can be a help. Through LinkedIn Premium, you can use a suite of tools —such as LinkedIn's AI program— to suggest edits to your profile that will ensure it is fine-tuned to reach your target audience. (And if you don't want to pay for Premium that's fine as well. Just use the free 30-day trial that LinkedIn offers and use Premium to spruce up your profile.) LinkedIn Premium's AI will help ensure your headline and "About" section tell the right story about your career.

3. **Periodically Share Quality Content (And Don't Overshare)**

   Be careful about the content you decide to share on your platform. As a rule of thumb, I only share content that:

   - Provides my followers with important insights about a key industry issue
   - Summarizes big wins and achievements for my team in a way that's not arrogant or self-aggrandizing
   - Sparks a dialogue amongst my followers, as well as re-shares
   - Inspires

As we saw with my rock-star CEO friend, oversharing or posting overly personal content can be off-putting to others and can damage the brand you're striving to cultivate in the long run. As a personal rule, I also avoid politics and other controversial topics on LinkedIn. I think of this platform as an extension of my corporate office. And if I don't discuss something in my office, I certainly won't discuss it in a public forum.

The Three Relationships You Need to Cultivate Now

1. **Your Boss' Boss**

   In a perfect world, it'd be enough for your great work to speak for itself. But corporate America doesn't work that way. You want to ensure that upper management is aware of the value you bring to the organization and how your work is helping the company achieve its goals. You want to be on the radar of your boss' boss when decisions are being made on who to promote, or which initiatives the company is going to pour resources into. If there's a plum assignment they need someone to lead, your name should be on the shortlist. But you won't accomplish any of this if your boss' boss doesn't even know who you are. You've got to be strategic about the relationships you build, and this is one of the most critical ones.

2. **Your Manager's Peers In Other Departments**

   Building a relationship with your manager's peers provides a wide range of benefits that will boost your career in the long run. For starters, you want as many friends in high places as you can get because it will increase your influence in the organization. These are the types of allies you'll need as you develop ambitious projects that will need cross-departmental support. Beyond that, getting to know your boss' peers will provide you with a more holistic understanding of the organization. These are the folks who will have crucial intel on the organization's strategic direction and future plans. And from a career development perspective, your manager's direct colleagues just might be the people who can connect you to that next opportunity.

3. External leaders outside your company

Regardless of where you work, it's important to keep your ear to the streets. You want to be up to date on the latest industry trends and best practices. No matter what level you are in the organization, you also want to be a rock star employee with big ideas that can transform your company. Or at the very least, help them remain competitive through innovation. Maintaining relationships with leaders beyond your company can be a great source of ideas. It's also a way to stay updated on important industry intel. If you're on the lookout for the next opportunity, these are the folks in your vast network who might just be able to plug you into the opportunity you seek.

CHAPTER EIGHT

THE MONEY CHAPTER - UNDERSTANDING YOUR WORTH, NEGOTIATING SALARY, AND GETTING ON A PATH TO GENERATIONAL WEALTH

"The racial pay gap is a persistent reminder of how systemic racism operates in the economy, denying Black workers the full value of their contributions."

—Ta-Nehisi Coates

On a fateful Monday morning in July 2017, Jamal called for an urgent meeting with his manager. The 34-year-old integrated marketer was fed up with his job. He was just shy of six months into his new role with a West Coast investment bank, and after a string of 70-hour work weeks, he had decided enough was enough.

That Monday morning was the day that Jamal was going to call his manager's bluff. He was doing the job of three people for less pay than what he believed to be his true market value and decided the time had come to push for a raise. Jamal also happened to be armed with some leverage. He had a solid job offer in his back pocket thanks to an old boss who was trying to recruit him.

Six months earlier, Jamal had been eager to escape from his less-than-satisfying role with a rival bank when he saw the perfect job description for his current role. On paper, it appeared to be the perfect position, and the stars seemed to align after Jamal cruised through four rounds of job interviews. It was a brutal punch to the gut when the new job offer came, to see there would be a 12% cut in his base pay with no room for negotiation. Against his better instincts, Jamal decided to accept a pay cut in exchange for the opportunity to have an exciting new job, which appeared a perfect fit for him. Within months, and now, under a crushing workload, while earning less for his labor, it was clear to Jamal that he'd made a mistake. He could do the work, but Jamal knew his value and decided it would have to be for what he was worth.

"I wanted to let you know that a former manager of mine reached out and offered me a job for $40,000 more than I'm making now," Jamal told his stunned boss. "Although I have a vision for how I can continue to do this job more effectively, I can't justify accepting less than my market value. I just can't. Are you able to be competitive with this offer? Because if not, I'm going to have to take it."

Jamal ultimately succeeded in earning a $40,000 raise from his current employer and didn't need to jump ship after all. But it did take him some time to recover from the stress of that high-stakes gambit.

Why Black Men Earn Less Than Their White Peers

Without realizing it, Jamal was swimming upstream against structural forces that have impacted Black people for centuries. Although it's been nearly sixty years since the Civil Rights Act was passed, there continues to be a significant wage gap in the United States across racial lines. Black men today earn roughly 87 cents for every dollar a

White man earns,[90] and this wage gap compounds with interest over time. Throughout a lifetime, Black men can expect to earn $1 million less than White men, a disparity that cumulatively has diverted an estimated $2.7 trillion away from Black America in the last two decades alone.

After achieving social and political gains in the decade following the Civil Rights Movement, Black men have made no progress in narrowing the wage gap with White men since 1980[91], a disparity that researchers attribute in part to an educational achievement gap. But even among men with the same college education as their White counterparts, research shows that Black men earn roughly 80% of the hourly wages that White men take home.[92]

Looking at Jamal's case, on paper it seemed like he'd done everything right. He completed a bachelor's degree with honors from a top university and polished his education off with an MBA from a respected program. He established a strong foundation for his career by landing a well-paying job with a top firm after completing his MBA. So why did he find himself underpaid? Beyond that, why should he feel a need to compromise, and accept less than his true market value to begin with?

Both Jamal and his manager, who is White, were unwittingly repeating an unfortunate history that has unfolded in U.S. corporate offices for generations. Black talent, usually not in a seat of any power or influence, is at the mercy of their White employer to bring them on an equal footing with their peers. This is what systemic racism looks like. Distinct from overt or outright discrimination, it is a purely structural phenomenon that Duke sociologist Eduardo Bonilla-Silva

---

[90] Payscale, "Racial Wage Gap for Men," May 7, 2019.
[91] Pew Research, "Racial, gender wage gaps persist in U.S. despite progress," July 1, 2016.
[92] Pew Research, "Racial, gender wage gaps persist in U.S. despite progress," July 1, 2016.

says results in practices and behaviors that provide benefits for some groups at the expense of others.[93]

In the United States, the roots of systemic racism can be traced back to slavery and the Jim Crow era, when federal, state, and local governments institutionalized structural advantages for White Americans at the expense of Black Americans. These policies resulted in racial disparities across virtually every walk of American life and impacted wages, wealth accumulation, educational outcomes, employment rates, incarceration rates, life expectancy, and more. Although the Civil Rights Movement succeeded in removing overtly racist laws from America's books, it stopped short of providing remedies for the damage less overt government policies have caused for generations.

Those disparities in American life still exist today, and they're a big reason why Black men have achieved little progress in narrowing the wage gap—even when they're educated and just as qualified.[94] Dr. Derek Avery, the C.T. Bauer Chair of Inclusive Leadership at the University of Houston, has done extensive research on racial inequality in the workplace. He attributes the racial pay gap to a variety of factors—ranging from a lack of Black people in positions of power and influence in American companies, to lower peak pay expectations from Black talent than what their White peers expect.

Reservation wage is a term that labor economists use to pinpoint the lowest wage rate for which a worker would be willing to accept a particular type of job. Reservation wage expectations are typically driven by household or family wealth, and today, the average White family possesses ten times the net worth of the average Black family.[95] So it should surprise no one that White employees almost universally have higher reservation wage expectations than their Black peers.

---

[93] Mashable, "What you need to know about systemic racism," June 29, 2020.
[94] Pew Research, "Racial, gender wage gaps persist in U.S. despite progress," July 1, 2016.
[95] Brookings Institute, "Examining the Black-White Wealth Gap," Feb. 27, 2020

One of the first things that you should do when entering a particular field is determine what your reservation wage is. Or to put it bluntly, what's the minimum number you'd consider before taking a role? But this exercise isn't always an easy one, particularly if you happen to come from a lower socioeconomic background. Avery says a lack of access to social networks that can help us understand our true market value, as well as the unconscious biases of hiring managers, can sometimes put Black men at a disadvantage during the salary negotiation process. In his 2017 report: "Bargaining While Black: The Role of Race in Salary Negotiations," Avery argues that hiring manager biases can impact salary negotiations. In his report, Avery reveals that in experiments with equally qualified male candidates, biased hiring managers expected Black men to negotiate less than their White peers. And when they did negotiate, those managers were less willing to make concessions to them than their White counterparts. This added up to lower starting salaries for those Black men.

What makes this such a difficult challenge for Black talent to overcome is that most people are unaware of their biases—and the hiring managers in Avery's experiment almost certainly did not consider themselves to be racist. But even when these Black candidates tried to do the right thing in negotiating, they were penalized for it. Avery suggests that the results of this experiment show that whether they realize it or not, many people continue to endorse the old American social order—with Whites at the top and Blacks at the bottom. And these biases can have a dramatic impact on salary negotiations.

"If my expectation as a hiring manager is that as a Black man, you should be happy that I'm even looking to hire you, then that sets the bar really low," Avery explains. "So, when you start to negotiate for yourself, it's like, 'Whoa, wait a minute. I was expecting you to be happy with the first thing I offered you." This puts you in the difficult position of having to push harder in negotiations and be even willing to walk away from an offer you've worked so hard to get in the first place. Such calculus is especially difficult if you're a first-generation talent coming from a family with no history of corporate, professional, or entrepreneurial success.

"This is why systemic racism is such a difficult thing for people to get their arms around because it's not one or two things we can point to," Avery says. "It's all of these different things that are woven together, so even if you're able to navigate your way around this one thing—six other things are waiting to make sure you don't get yours."

Negotiating the way to pay equity

We've explored the historical reasons for the racial pay gap, but there are some strategies and techniques that can be leveraged to tilt the scales more in our favor. It starts with negotiation.

Broadly speaking, there are generally only two times when talent possesses real, tangible leverage over an employer. First, when the employer has prepared an offer and is looking to get you into the fold, and second when you've decided you're ready to move on and have another offer lined up.

If you're like Jamal, you've got leverage in the form of another offer. If you're more junior in your career, and perhaps seeking your first corporate position, this is less likely—but there are still some things you can do to maximize your earning potential.

Getting a written job offer from a would-be employer is exhilarating. It's good to be wanted and a job offer brings with it hope and possibilities for an exciting future. There's a feeling that, "Yes, I've made it." All that education, preparation, and hard work to get to this point is starting to pay off. But before you accept a job offer, industry experts broadly agree that there are several steps you should take to ensure you're compensated fairly—chief among them being that you should always negotiate. No matter your level in the organization, never accept the first offer to come your way. Prospective employers expect you to negotiate, and you're almost certainly leaving money on the table if you fail to do so.

This brings to mind a time when I was strongly considering accepting a position at a large financial services firm. I pushed hard during the salary negotiation process. I pushed the hiring manager so far that at one point he finally said, "Look, the next offer I come back to you with is the final offer. This isn't going to be like negotiating a used car. The number I bring back to you is it."

To my pleasant surprise, I succeeded in getting the number I was looking for. To get there, I'd asked for $20,000 more than the number I was truly aiming for and had to be willing to take the negotiation to its absolute limit.

Particularly in cases like Jamal's, Avery states, there's a faulty reasoning that many candidates resort to. "You're like, 'Ok, the first offer is just the first offer. I'll get my foot in the door and I'll make it up.' But we know from the research that you don't ever make it up. Not only do you start lower, but it compounds over time. So, you end up being further and further behind by not starting at a more similar point to the White guy down the hall."

Chad Bennett, a human resources expert who owns a talent, diversity, equity & inclusion firm, says he's seen the scenario Avery describes play out countless times amongst Black men during his time in the HR space. "So many of us have this mindset that we should be grateful that we were even given an offer," Bennett says, "That we should accept what comes our way because we don't know when we're going to be given another opportunity to get this type of offer again." The mindset that Avery and Bennett are describing here is the "scarcity mindset," which the psychologist Dr. Shahram Heshmat says orients our minds "automatically and powerfully" to unmet needs.[96]

The scarcity mindset makes far too many of us eager to jump at the first offer that's thrown our way, and reluctant to negotiate confidently out of fear that the opportunity can easily be snatched away. "It's a mode of survival," Bennett says.

---

[96] Psychology Today, "The Scarcity Mindset," April 2, 2015.

The scarcity mindset has also led many of us to have lower expectations than our White peers of what we're worth. A 2000 study published in the Journal of Business and Psychology noted that White Americans have higher peak pay expectations than Black Americans for all job types.

Although this research is more than twenty years old, experts broadly agree that it still holds true.

Looking back at my own experience, I carried little sense of entitlement into my professional career after graduating from university. I was the son of a lower-middle-class family from pre-gentrified Brooklyn and there was only one thing I was certain of coming out of college: that I'd have to pay back the tens of thousands of dollars I borrowed to cover the cost of college. I was aggressively on the hunt for a solid entry-level job, and I was happy to take any reasonable opportunity that came my way to pay those bills on time.

Negotiating salary couldn't have been farther from my mind. In fact, throughout the early years of my career, I never negotiated and generally took the first offer without ever thinking twice. I didn't realize that I lacked an understanding of what my market value truly was or that negotiating salary was even possible. It wasn't until I met a young woman named Anika Dill when I was in my late 20s that my perspective changed. We met at a Brooklyn house party and eventually began dating. Early on in our relationship I was excited to get a job offer from ABC News and was ready to immediately accept it without thinking twice. "But aren't you going to even bother negotiating," I remember Anika asking me, incredulous at my ignorance. "Even in my first job out of college, I managed to squeeze out an extra few grand by negotiating. You're cheating yourself if you don't."

(Today we're married with three children.)

Beyond salary, which is the most critical component of your compensation package, there are other things you can sometimes negotiate, including work-from-home arrangements, stock options or restricted stock units (RSUs), vacation, and in some cases even your job title. At the executive level, Bennett says it's important to get legal counsel in assessing a compensation package as well. Additionally, consider what other benefits are important to you. Perhaps you need more flexibility built into your schedule or want the ability to volunteer but not necessarily have that deducted from your time off. You'd be surprised what you're able to build into your compensation package by simply asking.

Understanding Your Worth

As you head into salary negotiations, you must have a clear sense of what a particular role at a particular organization should pay. Platforms like Glassdoor, LinkedIn, and PayScale can be helpful, but to effectively research what others are earning for similar roles, it's important to cultivate a strong network of contacts within your industry.

For example, if you're a pharmaceutical marketer, make sure you know at least 10-15 other pharmaceutical marketers. It doesn't matter where these folks are located—they can be headquartered anywhere from L.A. to Omaha. These are the people who are going to help you understand both the ceiling and the floor for what you should be earning depending on the market you plan to work from.

If you happen to be fresh out of school and just starting out, it's critical that you prioritize building your network of industry peers and mentors. Over time, these will be the people who will provide you with useful intel on what your market value is. But remember, as a Black man, there's also an important catch to this strategy. You must make sure you have industry relationships beyond your community. "If you're talking to five other Black men, you all could be in the same bucket," Bennett explains. "So, you need to talk to a White male but also talk to a White woman, Asian, Indians—talk to people of all races if you can. Develop a list of contacts that you can reach out to, to understand what the market looks like."

In addition to salary, these types of contacts will also be able to provide intel on things like what your stock options should look like at a certain level and what your long-term incentives should be. Many companies use long-term incentives as a perk to reward employees for reaching specific goals that lead to increased shareholder value. The higher you climb the corporate ladder, the more important it is to get these types of insights from trusted peers. Leaning into trusted social networks to crowdsource information about compensation and other perks is crucial, once again, especially if you are the first of your family to successfully break into the corporate world.

"Having a strong social network is huge," Avery says. "Let's say I'm the first in my family to get an MBA in accounting. I don't have those deep connections who can tell me, 'You need to make sure your signing bonus is right and that they're throwing you variable compensation on top of that.' These are things that many of us never heard because of the circles we grew up in."

Break The Salary-Sharing Taboo Once And For All

Although strong social networks are essential to understanding your market value, their benefits are greatly undermined by corporate cultural taboos on discussing salaries with peers. Looking back at my own experience, there's always been an implied culture at nearly every company I've worked in that you simply don't discuss what you're earning with your colleagues. It's a taboo discussion topic in office settings, right alongside religion and politics.

Although non-union American workers have a right to share salary information with each other according to the National Labor Relations Act which was passed in 1935, U.S. companies have helped to foster a culture of secrecy on the topic of employee compensation. It's so ingrained in our work culture that many companies don't even see a need to forbid it outright—employees enforce it themselves.

In Feb. 2020, *The New York Times Magazine* noted that "employers, historically, have tried to stop information about employees' pay from escaping into the wilds of their offices because it might be harnessed and turned against them, and because its ultimate effects on the bottom line and on employee morale is unpredictable."

However, experts say a willingness amongst workers to share salary information is critical to closing pay gaps across both racial and gender lines. Breaking this taboo, however, is far easier said than done. It requires a willingness to be open and vulnerable with others, something that doesn't always come naturally. (But as noted in the prior chapter, building meaningful friendships with colleagues across multiple levels within your organization can be a huge help in this process.)

To understand the impact that discussing salary with peers can have, Black men can look to the Black actress Octavia Spencer as an example. Spencer is well-known for her roles as a maid in the 2011 hit film, "The Help," and as a mathematician in the 2016 film "Hidden Figures." During her time filming "The Help," Spencer forged a close friendship with her co-star Jessica Chastain, who is White. Years later, while working together on a comedy, Spencer confided in Chastain that she was being grossly underpaid and believed she should be making at least five times what she was earning for the film. "I told her my story and we talked numbers and (Chastain) was quiet, she had no idea that that's what it was like for women of color," Spencer told Variety Magazine in 2018. Chastain subsequently took up the cause for her co-star, who was eventually paid the same amount.

This is a great example of what can happen when people are willing to just have the conversation. Even if you're a little gun-shy about diving into specifics about what you're earning, this approach can at least give you a view of where you should be.

When And How To Bring Up Salary During The Negotiation Process

In addition to crowdsourcing information from industry peers about your market value, there are several tactics you can deploy to help maximize your earning potential with a prospective employer. Up front, after you apply for a job or hear from a recruiter about an opportunity, the next step in the process is usually an initial phone screening with a company. During this conversation, HR is assessing whether your skills and compensation expectations align with their vision for the role.

Without showing all your cards and with tact, it's okay to ask what the company has budgeted for the position or what the pay range is. As of June 2024, eight states have laws on the book requiring employees to list their pay range for a role on any publicized job description. with five states weighing their own pay transparency proposals as of this writing. Working through a job recruiter or headhunter simplifies this process because in most cases they would be the ones negotiating with the company on your behalf. Inevitably, the application or the hiring manager will ask the question: What are your salary expectations? It's at this point that you can provide a ballpark number for what you're looking for. You'll base this figure on all the information you've gleaned from industry contacts about what you should be earning for your level. Avoid giving a range here and instead offer a number that's well above where you'd like to be. If you give them a range, you'll almost certainly get an offer that's towards the lower end of it, if not the absolute bottom.

"As the employer is qualifying you, you need to be qualifying the employer," Bennett explains. "Be very clear at the beginning of the process when you're asked because it will come up: What are your salary expectations? Be firm on what you're looking for." Prospective employers also often ask about your salary history, which gives them insights into your reservation wage and a bargaining advantage during negotiations. But pay history questions for job applicants help perpetuate the cycle of race and gender-based pay discrimination, and they have been outlawed in nineteen states, including New York, Maryland, Illinois, California, North Carolina, and Michigan, as well as numerous big cities like St. Louis, Cincinnati, and Salt Lake City. (You can look up such laws in your state and locale on websites like Salary.com and HRDive.com)

As you move on from initial phone screenings and into subsequent interviews, put salary on the back burner for a moment and really dig into your specific questions about the role, your potential fit within the company, and what the work culture is like. An HR executive in the financial services space said that one of the biggest mistakes she routinely sees candidates make is bringing up compensation early on in the discussion with hiring managers. "You'd be shocked how often that happens," she said. "Like my goodness—you want to know about the salary without really knowing anything about the role? That's a major red flag and one of the biggest missteps that I see candidates make all the time."

Another mistake that candidates often make, this executive says, is when the dialogue shifts to compensation, they'll just throw numbers out there without any validation of why that's what they're looking for. "Every person in the HR space is going to have to justify why you deserve that extra $20,000 you're asking for, whether it's in the budget or not. This is negotiating. You don't just throw numbers out there. You've got to keep it factual and justify why you deserve that number."

Establish Your Target And Then Ask For More.

Once you've established the number you'd like to close on, it's important to push beyond that—even if it makes you a little uncomfortable. "In my career, I have negotiated 25% more than I was making in the previous role because I knew my market value," Bennett says. "I knew what the role was looking for, and I was so grossly underpaid where

I had been, that when I got the offer I still negotiated—even after I got my target number."

In a scenario where you've been given your target number on the first offer, it's possible that your expectations for the role were too low. "Having the courage to ask for more is important because this approach from the employer suggests they probably have more room in the budget for your role," Bennett says. If you fail to push harder in this case, you will almost certainly have left money on the table.

As with any type of negotiation, it's also important to know when to walk away. The goal here is to land an offer that you can be happy with and not make compromises that are going to hurt your earning potential over the long term. In Jamal's case, one could reasonably argue that he should have walked away from that 12% pay cut. He rationalized it and thought it was the right move, but within six months he was fed up and ready to move on again. It takes confidence to walk away but knowing your worth will help you exercise your BATNA options. BATNA is a negotiation technique that stands for Best Alternative to Negotiating an Agreement that was coined by William Ury and Roger Fisher in their 1981 book *Getting to Yes: Negotiating Agreement without Giving In*. Sometimes you just have to walk away if it is the best alternative.

Do your homework to understand what your market value is and don't accept a penny less than your research-driven target number. If the offer doesn't meet your goal, don't be afraid to walk. There are other companies in town.

Turning Your Wages Into Wealth

We've outlined some negotiation strategies and tactics to help maximize your earning potential, so now it's time to take a step back and ask an important question. What's the point of maximizing your salary if you're not leveraging it to get yourself on a pathway to long-term wealth accumulation? The object of the game here is to not only earn enough to comfortably pay your expenses, but to build wealth for you and your family.

You've succeeded in landing the job and negotiating the salary you want. Now it's time to put that money to work. In speaking with several financial advisors for this chapter, and from knowledge gleaned from more than a decade working in the financial services space, I've learned some basic rules of thumb to follow to maximize your savings and put your money to work for you. Here's a snapshot of how to approach your finances and maximize the return on the investment you've made in your career.

Entry-level Employee: Early-to-Mid 20s

Congratulations! You've completed your education and have succeeded in landing your first job out of school. Welcome to the real world. The first consideration for someone at your stage of life isn't necessarily about how to save—which is still important but managing the money you make effectively. Instead, your focus here should be on establishing a budget and not overcommitting yourself to big-ticket expenses.

"The most important thing at this level is to make sure you're living within your means so that you can start setting aside money for savings," said one financial advisor who I spoke with. "Then, assuming you've met the basic criteria of not spending more than you bring in—make sure that you begin putting money into your company's retirement plan. Whether it's a 401(k), 403(b), or TSP plan—whatever is, make sure you're putting money into it."

At a minimum, financial advisors say you should save a percentage of your salary up to wherever your employer will match you. For example, if the employer is going to match your savings up to three percent, don't contribute less than three percent. The company is giving you free money, and by not taking advantage of this benefit, you're giving it away. Additionally, most company retirement plans will allow you to incrementally increase the amount you're saving every year automatically. "Realistically, the likelihood of your paycheck getting bigger every year is high, so you probably won't even feel this extra contribution on your part," the advisor said.

After setting a proper budget for yourself, be sure to pay yourself through retirement savings and take advantage of a crucial asset that you have on your side at this stage of life: time. Those savings will add up and compound over time, as we'll explore later.

The Young Professional: Mid 20s to Mid-30s

For young professionals at this phase of their lives, an advisor I spoke with says he anchors the advice he delivers to clients on one key tip: "Always be buying" into the stock market. For young Black professionals who don't happen to come from independently wealthy families, the primary vehicle that they'll leverage to gain exposure to the capital markets is their company retirement savings plan. "If you're contributing to your 401(k)—no matter what your contribution is, whether it's three percent, five percent, 10 percent—you're always buying," he explains. "Every few weeks, you're either buying high or buying low—but the bottom line is, you're buying."

Financial advisors broadly agree that a standard company 401(k) plan will be your best-performing asset and that it's critical to be consistent with your savings. In a nutshell—just set it and forget it. Additionally, ensuring that you have diverse exposure to the market through your savings plan is also critical. "You should be buying the stock index through your plan," another advisor said. "When you're thirty years old and saving in a 401(k), there's not a lot of reasons to buy a bond, especially in today's environment. There's zero reason to be owning bonds in your retirement account because you're not going to touch that money for at least three decades."

At this phase of your career, it's important to still recognize that time continues to be on your side. Looking back at the last half century of stock market performance, there has never been a single thirty-year period when stocks were down. Not one. There's not even a single ten-year period when the stock market is down. "Unless you've got an inheritance, or decent savings at this point ranging between $100,000 and $300,000, your best investment option by far is your 401(k)," another advisor said. "Put as much as you can into it. It doesn't make sense to do a whole lot else."

You're still early in your career and probably around now dreaming of milestones like starting a family and homeownership. Save what you can afford to save as you keep these long-term goals in mind.

The Seasoned Pro: Mid-30s to Mid-40s

Life starts coming at you fast at this level, and if you're fortunate it'll come with such blessings as children and homeownership. You're now at a point where you're likely to be earning solid money. This means you should be able to afford to contribute the maximum allowable to your 401(k).

The IRS allows you to set aside up to $23,500 a year pre-tax through retirement savings plans. If you've been disciplined at this point about contributing to your plan, you'll start to notice that your balance is increasing nicely. "When you're putting more than $20,000 every year into your 401(k) and then your employer puts in an additional $7,000—$12,000, after 10 years you're looking at $300,000 to $400,000 in your account after contributions," an advisor told me. "That could very well be a $700,000 portfolio with market gains."

Now, allow yourself to imagine what your portfolio will look like if you save this way over a 30- or 40-year career. I know a number of 401(k) millionaires who are in their 40s who've managed to steadily contribute to their accounts for twenty years.

Advisors say that at this stage, your time horizon is still at a point where you should primarily be invested in stocks. But as you get deeper into your 30s and enter your 40s, you're now facing a whole new world of budgeting issues. This includes the costs of those blessings I mentioned —such as mortgage payments, childcare expenses, and saving for a child (or three) to go to college. But it's vital that you go beyond just saving what you can afford to as you did earlier in your career. The time has come to save to the max. Also—NEVER exit the market. Unless a disaster strikes in your personal life, stay invested if you're able to. "People really do underestimate the 401(k) and don't take it seriously enough," the advisor added. "So many people just don't contribute to their 401(k). They give money away by not contributing up to the company match, or they leave a job and cash out instead of rolling it over and staying invested. Then they're forced to pay taxes on it—and just like that, it's gone."

Withdrawals from a 401(k) before you turn 59½ come with a 10% penalty, on top of your normal income taxes. It's a painful hit, both on your near-term tax bill and in the gains you'll miss out on in the future. There are limited circumstances where withdrawals may be exempt from such penalties, but advisors almost universally agree that you should never tap retirement account savings unless it's absolutely necessary.

The Home Stretch: Mid-40s to Early 60s

When you're in your mid-to-late 40s, you're still in the thick of budgeting for all those big-ticket expenses that hit at mid-life. For many Black families, this could mean caring for aging parents who don't have wealth of their own. You're also probably covering the cost of college as well, which happens to come with a significant tax benefit. But at this point, you've still got to keep your eyes on the prize—and continue to max out your retirement savings.

As you enter your 50s, retirement is now on the horizon and the advisors I spoke with for this chapter broadly agree that your focus at this point should be twofold. First, you've got to make sure you have a retirement plan. And this plan goes back to the basics that you covered at the beginning of this journey. It's all about budgeting. Secondly, the time has come to focus on clearing debt from your balance sheet. "No one historically pays off their mortgage—very few people actually get rid of it," one advisor said. "But when you're going into retirement, you shouldn't have three car notes, and you shouldn't have $50,000 in credit card debt. You shouldn't have personal loans."

As you get deeper into your 50s, these types of debts should be dwindling to the end of their lifecycle. You should also have a firmer grasp of your budget and understand how much you're bringing in versus how much you're spending. As you prepare for retirement, you'll be able to assess what your income needs will be based on what your expenses are. The lower your expenses are, the easier a time you'll enjoy in retirement. Most people today survive in retirement off of Social Security and personal savings. If you've succeeded in steadily contributing to your 401(k) you should have a nice nest egg saved up for yourself at this point.

If you're still working in your late 50s to early 60s, your investment portfolio should be more conservative than it was when you were younger. "Your 50s is really about debt elimination," one advisor told me. "You should still put money into your 401(k) assuming you're still working. But the risk exposure should be slightly more moderate, such as 75% stocks and 25% bonds or cash because now you're looking at a 10-to-20-year time horizon. You also want to account for the risk of a crazy year like 2008 happening in the markets right before you retire so you're not fully crushed by it."

Building generational wealth is the goal

In an ideal world, at the end of your savings and investing journey, there should be a nice nest egg waiting for you. You've survived the gauntlet, and if you've managed to save consistently you should be able to enjoy your golden years in a state of financial independence. You should even be in a position to assist the next generation in building wealth by helping with things like down payments on first homes and covering the cost of college. To put this in perspective, consider what one advisor told me, "Let's say you've managed to accumulate $1 million into your 401(k). The safe bleed rate for those funds is about five percent a year," he said. "This means that you can safely pull $50,000 a year from that account, plus Social Security to live off of in retirement without any risk of running out of money. That's simple math."

And if you've got $2 million saved? The advisor said that amount doubles, and $100,000 can be pulled from the account every year, with no risk of you running out of money when this is supplemented by Social Security. At those amounts, there should be a lot left over to help the young people in your life, while enjoying the fruits of a lifetime of labor.

Unfortunately, research shows that far too many Black Americans—even the high earners among us—aren't on track for this type of payoff in retirement because we're not gaining enough exposure to the stock market and the types of risk assets that historically generate exponential growth over time.

Only 66% of Black Americans even participate in their company's 401(k) plan, compared to 77% of Whites, and we're more likely than any other group to take out loans or hardship withdrawals. As Mellody Hobson, co-CEO and president of Ariel Investments told Investment News, "Race is the No. 1 predictor of 401(k) plan participation." Just a third of Black Americans today even have a plan for saving for retirement[97] and a 2019 Federal Reserve study revealed that only 33.5% of Black households own stocks compared to 61% of White households. These disparities even exist among the wealthiest 5% of Black Americans. Wealthy Black families own less in stocks and bonds, and more in limited-upside assets like CDs, savings bonds, and life insurance.[98]

As a result, the racial wealth gap is widening, and by 2053, according to one estimate, the median wealth for Black Americans will fall to $0 if we don't reverse the current trend.[99] A key reason why White families succeed in accumulating generational wealth is they're twice

---

[97] Massmutual, "2018 State of the American Family Study."
[98] Credit Suisse, "Wealth Patterns Among the To 5% of African Americans," Nov. 20, 2014.
[99] Institute for Policy Studies, "The Road to Zero Wealth," Sept. 11, 2017

as likely to receive a life-changing inheritance or gift from elders than Black families.[100] Their inheritances are also three times larger than that of Black families.[101]

The only way to change this is by adopting a generational mindset and thinking beyond our lifetimes when it comes to personal finances.

Back in my early 20s, when I was just starting on my career path, I sought help from trusted elders with basics like building a budget, avoiding unnecessary debt, and getting on a pathway to homeownership. I also adopted a generational mindset from my grandmother, Constance Simpson. She'd emigrated to the United States from Panama in the 1950s and didn't have much. She raised my mom and four other children in public housing in Brooklyn, New York. But along the way she managed to get an accounting degree from Hunter College and eventually earned a role as an internal auditor for the IRS. Eventually, she accumulated enough resources to buy property in Brooklyn in the early 1980s back when it wasn't worth much. But today my family enjoys some wealth thanks to her foresight. That property has also appreciated handsomely thanks to gentrification. Constance Simpson's approach to personal finances helped set her great-grandchildren up for a better life than she probably could have imagined.

In our society people who inherit wealth are at an advantage over those who don't, and too many Black Americans continue to be disadvantaged on this front. Closing the racial wealth gap on a societal scale requires bold, visionary policy solutions from lawmakers and people of influence across the public and private sectors. But on an individual level, each of us has the power to effect change and the steps outlined here can help us put our families on a pathway to building intergenerational wealth.

---

[100] Economic Policy Institute, "Receiving an inheritance helps white families more than black families," Feb. 17, 2017

[101] Economic Policy Institute, "Receiving an inheritance helps white families more than black families," Feb. 17, 2017

CHAPTER NINE

ENDURING THE DREADED REORG (AND LAYOFFS) AND LIVING TO TELL ABOUT IT

"Control your destiny or someone else will."

—Jack Welch,
former Chairman & CEO of General Electric, 1981-2001

Terrance, a forty-one-year-old corporate vice president, finally landed his dream job. He had grown bored after more than fifteen years working in finance and investment-related roles. In the aftermath of George Floyd's murder, he was seeking career opportunities that would enable him to focus his professional efforts on the Black community while still earning a decent income.

Terrance's timing in pursuing this new career path was perfect because it coincided with the explosion in corporate philanthropy aimed at Black communities following the racial unrest of 2020. By October of that year, after less than three months of searching for a role, Terrance had landed a job at a large, publicly traded technology company leading philanthropic investments in underserved communities.

Beyond being a dream job, the role was a major step up for Terrance in terms of pay and influence. He had spent years in roles that were ultimately about creating wealth for institutional investors and wealthy families. Now, Terrance was in a different industry at the helm of a large-scale and high-profile effort to invest in communities in need—many of which, were Black. The role positioned him as a public spokesman for a major company for the first time, and the vast resources under his direction made him a key player both within the firm and with leading non-profit, government, and academic institutions.

A little over a year into the role, Terrance was starting to hit his stride. His strategy was finally fully baked, and the work left him feeling energized, empowered, and inspired. Just as he was settling into a smooth, operating rhythm, the company threw him a wicked curveball. They brought in a new executive to oversee its corporate philanthropy investments, which included Terrance's book of work. The hiring of this new executive included a full reorganization of Terrance's entire department and huge chunks of both the strategy and budget Terrance had been leading would now be split across several newly created teams. Terrance was also layered beneath a new, more junior boss than the managing director he had been previously reporting to.

These changes were a massive blow for Terrance, and to add insult to injury, he hadn't been directly informed by his manager about the new changes ahead. Instead, Terrance got the full story from a communications executive who'd reached out to him in advance of the press release and a firmwide announcement that was going out the following day.

"That was one of the most difficult days of my career," Terrance said. "I thought I had built a good rapport with my manager so to find out like this, felt like she had sold me up the river. I get that change in these companies is inevitable—it comes with the territory. But just the way it all went down, it was hard for me to stomach. It still is."

Living through reorganization is an unfortunate reality of corporate life. It can be a brutal experience that comes with layoffs, new bosses, and uncertainty about where you stand. Reorgs are morale killers, and they almost always cause losses in productivity as distracted, unsettled workers gossip and speculate about what the future might bring. Reorgs brought on by mergers and acquisitions can be even more painful since they bring the added fear of layoffs due to redundancies in roles and uncertainty over how to combine two formerly separate entities and cultures.

Why Do Companies Constantly Reorganize?

Companies almost always decide to change their organizational structures because something is broken. I've worked in corporate America for twenty years, and this has always been a common denominator for the dozens of reorgs I've experienced.

In some instances, company leadership decided a shakeup was in order because sales were down, or other important success indicators weren't being met. There've been times when someone senior left the company and the void created provided a chance for executives to evaluate things with fresh eyes. Then a new leader comes in and puts their stamp on things by shuffling the deck and creating their own org structure.

In other cases, market forces were the reason for the need to reorganize, either through a complete overhaul of business operations, or because of something more drastic—such as a merger with another company, or a sale of parts of the business. And then sometimes, there's a less dramatic reason for a reorg. I once managed corporate communications for a major asset manager, and we reorganized just about every six months to better align with the stakeholders our work supported.

Why Reorgs Are So Awful

> *"It's the not knowing—that's what's killing me."*
>
> —Michael Scott, The Office

Of all the childhood games I played in school classrooms growing up, musical chairs stand out the most because of how nerve-wracking it was. Around and around, we'd go. I would feel my heart pulsating and the adrenaline flowing as we walked in a tightly packed circle around a row of chairs while music played—until it didn't. The teacher would shut off the music and we'd try to sit down as quickly as we could—only there was a problem. There weren't enough chairs, and some poor kid would be left standing with nowhere to sit. Just like that, in the blink of an eye, they'd be out of the game. I never wanted to be the kid left without a place to sit. One of the worst parts about musical chairs is that it has virtually nothing to do with skill either. Although a little bit of athleticism can help, it's mostly about luck to find yourself with a chair to sit in when the music comes to its cruel stop.

Working in corporate America and going through a reorg is a bit like playing musical chairs. You spend your days going around and around in that metaphorical circle, doing your job until suddenly, the music stops. If you're fortunate, you'll find yourself in a good spot when this happens. It means you still have a job—or even a role that you still want to perform every day.

If you're less fortunate, perhaps your role has been eliminated, downgraded, or restructured into a new position that you don't want and didn't sign up for. Maybe, in a cruel twist of fate, you find yourself shifted away from a boss you like to a new leader you can't stand, or don't know very well. The worst part of reorgs, I've found, is the uncertainty they bring. Research shows that the uncertainty about the future that comes with reorgs can cause more stress and anxiety than the actual layoffs. Harvard Business Review notes that 60% of organizations experience a decline in productivity as they go through this process.[102]

---

[102] Source: Harvard Business Review, "Navigating Uncertainty About Your Role During a Reorg," Feb. 21, 2023.

As human beings, we've evolved to dislike uncertainty. Nature has designed our brains to be prediction machines. Our brains are constantly working to use our past experiences to help us position ourselves for favorable future outcomes.[103] On a primal level, we seek the comfort of knowing where that next meal will come from, and that we'll always have safe shelter to return to. Uncertainty throws our minds out of whack and weakens our ability to effectively prepare for the future.

Uncertainty is the root of all anxiety, and on a subconscious level, our brains expend tremendous energy trying to avoid it. Researchers have even found that uncertainty can cause more stress than inevitable pain. For example, a 2016 study found that people who knew there was a small chance of an electric shock could experience significantly more stress than knowing that they would definitely be shocked.[104]

> "When applying for a job, you'll probably feel more relaxed if you think it's a long shot or if you're confident that it's in the bag," says Dr. Robb Rutledge (University College London Institute of Neurology and Max Planck UCL Centre for Computational Psychiatry and Ageing Research). "The most stressful scenario is when you don't know. It's the uncertainty that makes us anxious. The same is likely to apply in many familiar situations, whether it's waiting for medical results or information on train delays."

Companies that are experiencing reorgs are fertile grounds for uncertainty, which is why restructuring typically negatively impacts staff well-being, regardless of whether or not their jobs are being axed.[105]

---

[103] Source: National Library of Medicine, "Uncertainty and Anticipation in Anxiety," July 2014.
[104] Source: UCL, "Uncertainty can cause more stress than inevitable pain," March 29, 2016
[105] Source: Science Daily, "Restructuring affects staff well-being regardless of job cuts," Feb. 1, 2016

Back in 2012, I lived through this type of uncertainty, and I wouldn't wish the fear and anxiety that it caused me on my worst enemy. At the time, I had a one-year-old daughter and wife to support. My wife was consulting part-time after losing her job due to the global financial crisis, and we were barely getting by on my modest income as the senior editor of a Wall Street news publication.

On a Monday in the fall of 2012, I showed up for work. As soon as I took off my coat, sat down at my desk, opened the Wall Street Journal website, and took that first sip of hot black coffee, the head of our division, Dave, approached my desk with a grave look on his face. "Hey Justin, can you join me for a sec over in the Central Park room," he asked. I could feel my skin flush, and perspiration began to form on my forehead. The acids in my stomach burned as I followed Dave toward the scenic conference room overlooking Central Park.

"We had to let Bryan go this morning," Dave said. Bryan had been my direct manager. "The company is beginning a broad restructuring of our editorial division and we'll no longer have the resources to support Bryan's role. You'll be in charge of the brand for the time being. I know this is a tough way to start the week, but you should see this moment as a growth opportunity. You're now the de facto Editor-in-Chief. We're excited for you."

There was no raise with this "promotion," just more work. The news left me numb. The next day we were hit with another shock, as the parent company announced it would be shuttering numerous publications within its stable, and that as part of a broad restructuring, was laying off hundreds of editorial, sales, and tech support staff.

That numb feeling I'd experienced when my manager got canned was quickly replaced by a sense of dread. Following the office bloodbath, I went home that evening and held my infant daughter. It made me sick, deep within my soul to look at her innocent little face and worry that I wouldn't be able to provide for her. Beyond that, the thought of her ever having to experience a day like the one I just went through filled me with a deep, existential sadness.

Despite my "promotion," this reorg left me feeling scared and powerless. The surviving leaders in the company tried to boost the morale of the remaining staff by taking us out for a swanky lunch at a trendy restaurant in Midtown Manhattan. But during that lunch, they couldn't provide us with any definitive answers on where the company was headed and whether the bloodletting would stop anytime soon.

So, I did what any sensible person in these circumstances would do. I spent a couple of hours the following day updating my resume and began blasting it out far and wide in search of work. My productivity nosedived in the days and weeks after that as I spent most of my time searching for jobs and going out for coffees and lunches with contacts who might be able to connect me with a role. I did as little work as I could to keep management off my back and treated that employer as if they were paying me to look for a new job. Most of my colleagues were doing the same.

I'll never forget the atmosphere in that office after the reorg and layoffs were announced. For weeks, it was as if dark storm clouds had shown up and cast a pall over the entire building. The mood was funereal. And in a cruel twist, they didn't immediately let my old manager Bryan go after telling him his job had been eliminated. Instead, they told him they needed him to stay on for another few weeks. These were the days before remote and hybrid work, so Bryan had to show up, day after day, and awkwardly face the people who fired him. Bryan, a White man, was dealing with even more difficult personal financial circumstances than what I was managing. He was a recovering alcoholic in his late 40s and had three children, the youngest of whom is autistic. His wife's income as a physical therapist helped, but they were living paycheck to paycheck like many Americans. It must have been a sad sight for those in the know watching him interact with the people who let him go for those final few weeks. Dutifully he trudged in every day, never letting them rob him of his dignity.

"Rhonda burst into tears as soon as I told her the news," Bryan said of his wife's reaction to his layoff. "No one here will even look me in the eye anymore either. Bastards."

Learning To Live With Ambiguity

"Maturity is the capacity to endure uncertainty."

—John Huston Finley,
20th-century American educator and author

One of the first lessons I learned during the formative years of my professional life is that if you work in corporate America, you're going to have to accept uncertainty. I saw early on that the appearance of stability is an illusion, and that you can show up for work on any given day, only to be told your services are no longer needed.

Friday, Feb. 6, 2004, was this type of nightmare day for 80 corporate and administrative employees at Madison Square Garden (MSG), whose parent company at the time, Cablevision, owned the New York Knicks and New York Rangers.[106] Although it was still a money-making machine, MSG hadn't been as profitable in recent years as it had been during the 1990s, when the Knicks and Rangers were both mainstays in the playoffs and regularly competed for championships. By 2004, both teams were mired in a long stretch of mediocrity and missed the playoffs with regularity. This hurt MSG's bottom line because the company counted on gate receipts and other revenues that came from both teams qualifying for the postseason.

For years, investors had been growing antsy about the company's lagging performance and there were even rumors that Cablevision could be a buyout target from an activist investor. To help find the solutions its investors craved, MSG brought in the consulting firm

---

[106] Six years later, Cablevision spun off its MSG properties, including its sports teams into the Madison Square Garden Company.

McKinsey & Company to assess what it could do better. McKinsey recommended sweeping layoffs and restructuring.[107]

As part of that restructuring process, MSG merged its sponsorship sales team with its marketing group—where Aaron, a junior-level associate worked.

"That was such a terrible day—I literally lost all three of my bosses in one day," Aaron says of the Feb. 6, 2004, layoffs. "Three different women, all senior. One minute, they'd be sitting at their desk only to get a call to go to a special room. Then I'd see them coming back to their desk, escorted by security. My main boss took it as well as anyone could in those circumstances. Working for the Garden had been her dream job. She said, 'welp, ok, this sucks, but that's life.' I helped her box up her stuff. We both cried, but she was gone within about an hour."

The big boss didn't take it well—at all. "She had been a Garden lifer," Aaron says. "It was a mess. She moved painfully slow to pack her stuff and get out of there. She was moving like you were kicking her out of her home. It got pretty awkward. She wound up staying the whole day, with security watching her every move the whole time."

Before those layoffs, there was cautious optimism that MSG was about to benefit once again from a winning Knicks team. Two months earlier, the Knicks brought in Isiah Thomas to overhaul its basketball operations, and shortly after that acquired all-star point guard Stephon Marbury in a massive trade.[108] But the writing was on the wall.

"We lost people that day who we thought were irreplaceable," Aaron says. "Everyone thinks they're indispensable, until of a sudden they're not. To this day, I swear this is why I'll never bring so much personal stuff into an office that I need a box if they ever let me go."

---

[107] Source: New York Post, Feb. 7, 2004: "Cablevision axes 80 at MSG"

[108] Both moves notoriously backfired, with the Knicks descending into a laughingstock for much of the last 20 years.

I began my career shortly before the Great Recession of 2008-09, in which 8.6 million Americans lost their jobs—my mom being one of them. She had been a longtime employee of Goldman Sachs, and she was among the thousands of workers they let go as a historically bad economy took a huge bite out of their profits.

Around that time, I was a stock market reporter for Thomson Reuters. My job was to talk to stock analysts all day and report on why the markets were moving in a particular direction. The most memorable story I wrote was a piece about the unofficial start of the Great Recession: the stunning collapse of the stalwart investment bank Bear Stearns. The company—which made Fortune's 2007 list of most admired companies the year before it collapsed—failed after making bad bets on subprime mortgage loans. The enduring memory for me of Bear Stearns was its thousands of dazed workers streaming out of its Madison Avenue headquarters with their belongings in a box, headed out towards an uncertain future.

Between my mom, wife, those laid-off Bear Stearns workers, and the millions of people who lost their jobs across the country during that dark time, I and my Millennial contemporaries saw that to work in corporate America meant that you didn't have control over your future. Those of us who were entering the workforce back then were stepping into a cold world where investors rewarded companies for mass layoffs and the offshoring of jobs with short-term boosts in the value of their stock.

As young people raised by the Baby Boomer generation, we were taught to work hard in school and get good grades to ensure we could land a decent job after graduating from college. This was especially important in a time when blue-collar manufacturing jobs were disappearing, while the so-called knowledge economy was coming to the fore. But the market crisis of 2008 made it painfully clear that we now lived in a time in which workers, even those with college degrees, couldn't always count on their job being there. The days of working in one job, for one company for thirty years before retiring to collect a pension and a gold watch, were a distant memory.

Instead, workers would now have to learn to live with ambiguity, which is especially difficult when you consider that there's nothing ambiguous about the need for health insurance, student loan payments, the mortgage payment that's due on the first of every month, or all the myriad expenses that come with raising a family—or even supporting yourself alone in an expensive city.

Quick History Lesson: A Time Before Nerve-Rattling Reorgs And Mass Layoffs

Imagine working for a company that paid enough for you to support a family of five on one income, provided generous cradle-to-the-grave benefits, and consistently generated so much revenue that it offered outlandish perks like lavish annual carnivals for families, country club memberships or free golf course access for all employees. At this company, no one ever got laid off, and if it ever needed to go through a reorg and eliminate jobs, they'd give you a chance to stay on by retraining you for a new role at your full salary. At worst, you'd have to explore moving to another part of the country or even overseas, but you never had the specter of a layoff looming over you.

With the stress of losing your job far from your mind, you could lean into your work, build confidence in your abilities, and focus on doing what it took to climb the ladder. Your connection to this company would run so deep that it would become part of your very identity. You were a company man, and your children would proudly tell their friends where Dad worked. This sounds like a fantasy, right?

Well, this was a reality throughout much of the 20th century at IBM, which was once one of the world's most admired companies. It was the Apple or Google of its day. It's hard to believe, but for more than 70 years, IBM never laid off its workers. In a nod towards the company's policy of retraining or relocating employees due to a need to reorganize, employees jokingly said IBM stood for "I've Been

Moved.[109]" IBM wasn't the only U.S. company to take this type of paternalistic approach with employees, either.

In the decades after World War II, the U.S. economy enjoyed a sustained period of exponential growth with virtually little overseas competition as the nations of Europe and Asia rebuilt after the war. American companies got a generous head start in the burgeoning global economy as we know it today, much to the benefit of both their shareholders[110] and the nation's labor force. This period, which coincided with the rise of the Civil Rights Movement, was the golden age of American capitalism. These were the halcyon days for American workers, and during this time, if you managed to land a job at a multibillion-dollar corporation like General Electric (GE), Xerox, Eastman Kodak, or even at one of the Big Three automobile manufacturers,[111] you had it made. As long as you worked hard and delivered value for the company, you could enjoy the type of job security and retirement benefits that we can only dream of now.

By the 1960s, IBM was arguably the most generous company in the nation in terms of the benefits and security that it provided for its workers. But Eastman Kodak wasn't that far behind. It provided a so-called wage dividend, which was an annual lump sum payment on top of your normal salary, as well as on-the-job training programs to help you expand your skill set. It even covered the cost of seventy-five percent of your tuition for courses that could help you advance your career. Unlike today, when most American retirees live in fear that they'll outlive the nest egg they spent decades of their lives building,[112] Eastman Kodak—like most companies back then—generously covered the cost of employee pensions. Here's

---

[109] Source: Marketplace.org, "IBM: when corporations took care of their employees," June 13, 2016
[110] Source: S&P 500 performance: 1945-1970
[111] Source: Investopedia, April 18, 2022
[112] Source: CNBC, "Retirees' biggest fear is outliving their assets, research finds. These tips can help." June 13, 2013

how the company explained the program in its 1960 handbook[113] for new employees:

> "From the day you start work, Kodak is building up a retirement annuity for you under the Company's Retirement Annuity Plan. That annuity becomes yours as an absolute right after you've been with Kodak for fifteen years, even though you were to leave the Company for any reason before reaching retirement age. Kodak's Retirement Annuity Plan provides for monthly payments when a person retires under its terms. Your payments will be based on your total earnings with the Company up to age sixty-five, and they will continue as long as you live. These payments are, of course, in addition to the government payments you may expect to receive under Social Security. Kodak pays the full cost of the Plan. You don't pay a cent."

There was just one problem with this idyllic environment that U.S. corporations provided for their workers. Black people—as well as women, Jewish people, and other racial minorities—were often systematically excluded from participating in it. Kodak, for example, didn't hire Black people or women.[114]

While IBM is doing a commendable job in the DEI space today[115]—most notably around its efforts to hire and promote Black workers—back then it reflected the corporate norms of its time.[116] This meant that the employees who developed its products were predominantly White and mostly male.

---

[113] Source: Eastman Kodak new employee booklet, 1960
[114] Source: The Atlantic: "The Rise and Fall of a Tech Giant," July/Aug 2021 issue.
[115] Source: Bloomberg, "OneTen Launches Pilot with Merck, IBM to Meet Million Jobs Goal," June 29, 2021
[116] Source: LA Times, "My father was IBM's first black software engineer. The racism he fought persists in the high-tech world today," Sept. 22, 2019

My grandmother, Constance Simpson, tried in vain to get a job at IBM in the mid-1960s after completing her accounting degree at Hunter College in New York. In addition to being a Certified Public Accountant (CPA), Mrs. Simpson had years of experience running payroll and bookkeeping for a small firm in the city. She had been delighted to get the opportunity to interview for an accounting position at IBM after completing a job application.

But when she showed up at IBM's office, my grandmother was greeted coldly by a secretary who appeared taken aback that a Black woman was there for a job interview as an accountant. "Oh, you must be in the wrong, place," the woman told my grandmother after she explained why she was there. After politely correcting the secretary, Mrs. Simpson was given a perfunctory interview with the hiring manager. Following that interview, my grandmother never heard from IBM again. Besides IBM, she applied for accounting jobs at numerous companies, only to be turned away left and right. It was a sign of the times. Until the 1970s, Black women were largely excluded from the better-paying, higher-status jobs that they can realistically compete for today.[117]

Eventually, Constance Simpson's persistence paid off, and a few years later she landed a role as an internal auditor for the Internal Revenue Service where she worked until retiring in the mid-1990s.

How did it come to this? The man who popularized mass layoffs

"I am not a destroyer of companies. I am a liberator of them."

—Gordon Gekko, *Wall Street*

By the 1970s, both affirmative action and the legal victories of the Civil Rights Movement had helped to force open the doors of opportunity for Black and other historically marginalized populations both within

---

[117] Source: Economic Policy Institute: "Black women's labor market history reveals deep-seated race and gender discrimination," Feb. 19, 2019

corporate America and at universities across the country. Doors that were once essentially shut to Black talent during the golden age of American capitalism were wedged open ever so slightly. The decade saw companies begin to set hiring goals for diverse talent. The Equal Employment Opportunity Act of 1972 signed by President Nixon gave the federal government greater powers to enforce against workplace discrimination.[118]

But while opportunity finally seemed to beckon for Black people in corporate America, a confluence of macroeconomic factors kept those opportunities in check. These weren't the boom years of the 1950s and 1960s that Black professionals were walking into. Instead, the 1970s were a decade when the U.S. economy began to slow to a crawl for a variety of reasons. Europe and Asia were finally open for business and their companies began competing on the global stage for the first time since the end of WWII. Meanwhile, oil price shocks hurt the economy by making energy much costlier for businesses and consumers, while inflation eroded the spending power of most Americans. Mass layoffs hit numerous blue-collar sectors during the 1970s, including manufacturing, construction, autos, and the steel industry.

By the 1980s, U.S. corporations were well on their way toward evolving into the cold-blooded money-making machines we know them to be today, with 1981 marking a crucial turning point. In 1981—months after Ronald Reagan began the first of his two terms in the White House—Jack Welch began his storied tenure as the chairman and CEO of GE. When Welch took the helm, GE was thriving. The company was the world's tenth largest in terms of market capitalization, was worth $14 billion, and employed 400,000 people. Its products touched virtually every aspect of American life, and its employees enjoyed lifelong careers, a living wage, and stability.

---

[118] Source: NixonFoundation.org, "Nixon's Record on Civil Rights." Aug. 4, 2017

But Welch demanded more, and he took a starkly different approach to leading GE than his predecessors. His approach would influence an entire generation of CEOs, and copycats would mimic his methods for the next forty-plus years.[119] He would also be widely celebrated for how he managed, and in 1999, was named Fortune's Businessman of the Century.[120]

Welch started his reign by overhauling GE's organizational structure through a series of dramatic reorgs and layoffs. Despite the company's good health, Welch laid off 72,000 people within his first two years at the helm and closed a dozen factories. Eventually, he required managers at the company to rank their employees in terms of performance and then cut the bottom 10%. By 1985, Welch had eliminated 100,000 jobs at GE. When he retired in 2001, Welch had slashed 170,000 jobs in all.

GE stock became a Wall Street darling as Welch pioneered such cost-cutting maneuvers as offshoring jobs and replacing long-time employees with less costly contractors. He capitalized on Reagan-era regulations by instituting frequent stock buybacks,[121] which further juiced the value of GE stock. After twenty years leading the company, GE had posted annualized share price growth of 21%, which outpaced the S&P 500 by far (even in bull markets.[122]) On the day before Welch took over GE, its shares were trading at $2.38 each. On the day he left, they were trading at $135.69, a 5,600% increase. In comparison, the S&P 500 rose 700% over the same timeframe.[123]

---

[119] Source: "The Man Who Broke Capitalism: How Jack Welch Gutted the Heartland and Crushed the Soul of Corporate America—and How to Undo His Legacy," by David Gelles, 2022
[120] Source: Fortune, Nov. 1, 1999
[121] A stock buyback is when a company buys its own outstanding shares to reduce the number of shares available on the open market. Companies do this for a variety of reasons, including to increase the value of their stock by limiting supply, and to also defend against other shareholders from buying a controlling stake.
[122] Source: MIT Management Review: "Did Jack Welch Blow Up the Business World?" Oct. 18, 2022
[123] Source: Yahoo Finance: "Jack Welch's GE legacy ended last week: R.I.P." March 15, 2023

It's hard to overstate Jack Welch's influence on corporate America today. His management style is a big reason why mass layoffs have been normalized, along with jarring reorgs. Welch trained more than thirty-five CEOs at some of the world's leading companies, and no doubt influenced others from afar. Before Jack Welch, the idea that a healthy company would axe the jobs of thousands of people was scandalous. Today, it's become the norm.

There's a human cost to being a corporate worker who is ultimately seen as disposable by their company. But there are strategies one can harness to prepare for the roller coaster life of a corporate employee without feeling diminished.

Conclusion: 9 Tips For Surviving A Reorg (Or Layoff) And Thriving In The Process

1. **Never Be Caught Off Guard. Understand The Environment You're Working In.**

   Even before your company reaches the stage where it's reorganizing or executing mass layoffs, you should have a sense of how healthy the business—and the industry it operates within—is. What did the company's latest earnings report reveal? What are the conditions of the market it's operating in? Both elements—no matter how solid your company may seem—are telltale signs of whether massive changes could be coming. For example, a good friend of mine was working for a large bank's home lending division in 2022 when there were indications that the housing market was cooling off. He sensed that layoffs wouldn't be far behind since there would be far fewer loans to process than a year before when tens of thousands of people were refinancing their mortgages or buying new homes in the COVID-era low-interest rate environment. By early 2023, as demand for mortgages cratered, his company quietly laid off over 1,000 employees and reassigned hundreds more.

My friend was one of the lucky ones. Thanks to his foresight, he managed to get transferred to a different business unit months before the changes began. "I called this one, didn't I!," he told me in a triumphant text message the day the changes went public. It wasn't a shock to him at all, or anyone else who reads the Wall Street Journal every day.

Staying informed and understanding the environment you're working in should give you plenty of lead time to make an informed, timely decision about your future before the storm hits. You can make your luck, like my friend did.

2. **Avoid The Office Rumor Mill.**

One of the guilty pleasures of working in corporate America is linking up with a trusted colleague to get the scoop on what's happening in the office. A little gossip can be a good thing in some cases. It can be devilishly fun to dish on what you've seen and heard, or even just vent to each other about the challenges you're dealing with. This type of gossip can help deepen the bond between teammates. It's a plus if your office besties are plugged into the latest happenings in the company because this can be another source of information in understanding the health and future of your employer. Sometimes, you can even find new opportunities through these types of conversations—if they're with the right people.

But beware of office gossip if your company is going through a reorg or mass layoffs. These are emotionally charged environments, which means there's a good chance the gossip network isn't a good source of accurate information. In uncertain work environments, people are scared, emotional, and angry—which means it's a good time to remember that you've got two ears and one mouth. Do more listening than talking and only focus on information that you receive from valid sources, like your manager or senior leadership. You can protect precious energy by avoiding too much commiserating with your frazzled teammates as well. These types of conversations will sap your physical, mental, and spiritual energy if you're not careful.

3. **Tap Into Your Network—Both Within The Company, And Beyond.**

   If you sense job-threatening changes are on the horizon (or they're already underway,) the time has come for you to begin having strategic conversations with your network. Don't be shy about letting folks know what you're experiencing and looking for. Be open and transparent. Instead of participating in energy-killing gossip, which is unproductive and ultimately serves no purpose, engaging your network is a way to give yourself control over your future. This is the time to stay visible. Get out there for coffee and lunches with the folks who can help you, and don't hesitate to reconnect with contacts you haven't spoken with in a while.

4. **Keep An Open Mind – And Be Flexible.**

   I once had the misfortune of winding up with a new boss that I couldn't stand after a reorg. She was a negative person who was difficult to work with and she was so unpopular that teammate after teammate expressed their sorrow for me suddenly having to report to her. I was furious the day I found out about the change and my first instinct was to begin feverishly applying for new jobs outside of the company. Almost immediately I wanted to take the first offer I could get and then give my new manager the proverbial finger on my way out.

   But after allowing myself exactly one day to be angry, I took a step back and analyzed my situation without emotion. I was in a job that held significant influence both within the company and beyond. I also liked the work, and it wasn't in my personal career roadmap to ditch the role just yet. There were still some goals I needed to accomplish and fortunately, my job was safe. So, I kept my head down and focused on doing the best work of my life. Six months later, an executive from another line of business in the company approached me about a role that represented a significant promotion. That opportunity transformed my career, and it would have never happened if I'd made an emotion-driven decision to leave the company prematurely. Coincidentally, that terrible boss didn't last another year, either. She was gently forced out after alienating one too many business partners.

It's okay to decide to buckle up and ride out the changes after a reorg. You can use this time to evaluate the direction the organization is headed in and to determine whether it aligns with your vision. There's no need to stick around if they're making changes that you don't believe will better the company.

5. Lean Into Self-Care.

Going through a layoff is one of the most stressful things a person can ever experience. One study found that a layoff is more stressful than a divorce, the death of a close friend, or even the sudden loss of your hearing or vision.[124] Going to work every day when you're uncertain about your job security is similarly awful. Both scenarios will take a toll on your physical and mental health if you're not careful. During times like these, it's easy to turn to cheap sources of short-term comfort that will seriously damage your health over the long term, such as junk food, alcohol (or drugs), binging on too much TV, and neglecting your workout routine.

---

[124] Source: National Library of Medicine: "The Life Events Inventory: re-scaling based on an occupational sample," June 2001

You need your body and mind to be sharper than ever to ensure that you can think clearly and feel good as you take control of your future. Prioritize getting enough sleep, drinking enough water, and putting healthy foods into your system. Support your mental health by spending time with close friends and family who nourish your spirits, cheer you up, and support you as you lay the groundwork for the next chapter in your life.

As part of your self-care routine, give yourself a moment to pause and think things through. Whether you've been laid off or dealt a bad hand in a reorg, take a step back and reflect on what's transpired. This is a moment to reassess what you truly want from your career. Times like these can be a blessing in disguise by providing a rare window for you to reinvent yourself and lean into areas that you're passionate about.

If you've been laid off

6. Negotiate Your Severance.

If you find yourself in the unfortunate position of being laid off, there are several steps you can take to position yourself for the best possible exit. For starters, don't feel compelled to immediately sign any severance documents that your soon-to-be former employer gives you. You've just been dealt a traumatic blow, and you need to give yourself a little time to process the news. In most cases, you're allowed up to three weeks (21 business days) to accept a severance agreement, and after you've signed it, you even have seven business days to change your mind.

You can negotiate remaining listed on your employer's website until you land a new job, which will enable you to not appear unemployed during your search. It's even possible to negotiate getting the company to cover the cost of your health insurance until you find a new role.

Employers are not legally required to pay laid-off employees a severance. But it's become standard practice for companies to provide you with two weeks of pay for each year you've been with them. You can negotiate how that package is paid out, such as asking for it in installments or one lump sum. You can potentially negotiate to get the company to pay you the unvested amount of your 401(k) and restricted stock units[125] (RSUs). The bottom line here, is you don't have to simply accept what's given to you. Push for as much as you can on the way out.

7. **Announce Your Layoff On LinkedIn.**

Believe it or not, one of the quickest paths to a new job these days after a layoff is by sharing the news publicly on social media. Although your instincts might tell you to hunker down and put on a brave face after the devastating loss of your job, in sharing your news publicly, you'll be setting the wheels in motion toward landing your next opportunity much quicker than you might expect. Your network will amplify your message. Key contacts will take note and refer you for roles, and even hiring managers will take note as well. Just don't bash your former employer on the way out. A gracious announcement is the way to go.

Consider the case of Mitch, who was the head of marketing for a major tech firm, when he was shockingly laid off on a Monday in July 2023. He shared the news of his layoff on LinkedIn, which prompted his network to quickly spring into action. "One of my former colleagues shared my post with one of his startup clients," he said. "Then a reporter commented

---

[125] Investopedia: "A restricted stock unit (RSU) is an award of stock shares, usually given as a form of employee compensation. The recipient must meet certain conditions before the restricted stock units are transferred to the owner.

on it and two CEOs reached out. I got two interviews with companies almost immediately. And then I got an offer to lead marketing at a startup exactly two weeks to the day I was laid off. It worked out. It's weird being out there and vulnerable. You hear from so many people. It's surprising."

8. **Build A New Routine.**

After losing your job, it's easy to feel directionless as well as experience a loss of purpose in your life. Jobs infuse structure into our days and reward us by providing challenges that enable us to feel accomplished. Without a job, you must create this structure for yourself. Perhaps this means you apply for a certain number of jobs every day or have a certain number of meetings with industry contacts every week. Maybe there's an entrepreneurial idea that you've been waiting for the right moment to launch. This can even be the time to get in the best shape of your life. You've suffered a big loss, but allowing yourself to score easy wins regularly is a way to rebuild your confidence as well as a sense of control over your life.

9. **Create A Plan For Health Insurance.**

Most workers in the U.S. rely on their employers for health insurance. But if you've lost your job, there are a few things you can do to ensure you still have coverage. For starters, research healthcare plans in the Affordable Care Act Marketplace.[126] These plans cover essential healthcare benefits, such as hospitalization, ambulatory patient services, emergency services, maternity and newborn care, prescriptions, rehabilitation services, pediatric services, lab tests, and preventive care—among other basic benefits. You may even qualify for a subsidy that

---

[126] The ACA Marketplace is a platform that offers insurance plans to individuals, families, and small businesses. Learn more at HealthCare.gov

will lower the cost of your monthly premium. The amount of your subsidy is based on your household income. There are some potential drawbacks to ACA plans, such as the need to ensure your current medical providers are in the network. You'll also need to double-check that your prescriptions are covered as well so that you don't get hit with expensive out-of-pocket costs.

A second option is COBRA coverage, which would allow you (and your spouse or any dependents) to remain on your former employer's plan after your job has been terminated. One positive about this approach is that it's the same plan you had under your old employer, and it can last anywhere from 18 to 36 months. This means you get to keep all your doctors and your prescriptions will still be covered. The downside is you'll now pay the full cost of the plan with no subsidy from your former employer, which means COBRA is expensive in the long run.

A third option is short-term medical insurance. These plans are sold through private companies. They provide coverage for a short period ranging from anywhere between three months to up to a year. Short-term plans are a cheap option, but they usually provide less coverage and fewer benefits than what you'll get from COBRA or the ACA Marketplace. Short-term health insurance providers will also ask you about your medical history and can deny you coverage for preexisting conditions.

CHAPTER TEN

MANAGING THRIVER'S GUILT

"In every conceivable manner, the family is a link to our past, a bridge to our future."

—Alex Haley

"**J**ustin—do NOT fall asleep," my brother Rick[127] screamed, with fear in his eyes as he squeezed my hand for dear life. "If you start to feel drowsy, let me know, but PLEASE, with all your strength, stay awake. You can't fall asleep, okay? I need you to give this everything you've got, kid."

I was strapped to a gurney in the back of an ambulance as it raced through Clinton Hill toward Downstate Medical Center, the hospital where I was born fifteen years earlier.

My older brother Rick was at my side, frantically trying to make sure I wouldn't fall into an eternal sleep. My little brother Max[128], sat on the opposite side of the gurney in stunned silence—with tears

---
[127] Name and details are changed to protect the person's identity.
[128] Names and details are changed to protect the person's identity.

welling in his eyes. At this point in my young life, Rick and Max were the two people to whom I was closest.

It was Labor Day weekend in 1995 and a steamy Brooklyn summer was coming to a close. In the minutes before I found myself in that ambulance with my life hanging in the balance, I was chillin' out on the block with a few homies and some around-the-way girls. The sun was setting, and the streetlights had just come on, which meant it'd be time for me to get home soon. The first day of school was the following week, and we were savoring our final days of freedom and warmth before the academic rat race began. It was the typical, boring August dog day when suddenly all hell broke loose—which was always a risk back then during Brooklyn summers. Where I'm from, warm weather and bored teenagers were a dangerous mix. And right before I was about to head home, our idyllic day nearly turned deadly.

For reasons that I still don't understand, my "friend" Charlie and I started horsing around—playfighting as our homeboys and the girls looked on. Charlie had given me a little shove, and I shoved him back—and we suddenly found ourselves grappling the way WWE wrestlers do at the start of a match.

Our little playfight started innocently enough, no different than two young rams butting heads. But like hot water rising from a simmer to a slow boil, the tension and intensity of our grappling increased. We weren't in an outright fight, but it was clear that we were both trying to get the better of each other in the exchange. We were a pair of 15-year-old boys, powered by raging hormones and growing egos, and neither of us intended to be the dude who got physically bested by another guy in front of all those onlookers—especially with girls on the scene.

Natalie was there, looking on, and because of her presence, I decided to go all out in my little scuffle with Charlie. Natalie was a petite, brown-skinned girl with long hair and pretty eyes, and I'd had a crush on her all summer. I reached out to grab Charlie by the neck. My plan was to grab him and then quickly end our little bout by squeezing him into a submission hold. Since I was the larger guy, I figured that once I had Charlie in my grip it would be game over, and our little tussle would be finished.

But for some reason, Charlie happened to have a box cutter in his right hand. And just as I grabbed at his neck, Charlie slashed at my torso with that box cutter. I then felt a searing pain tear through my chest. The pain seemed to bore right through me. Like a drill through drywall. My hands immediately dropped from Charlie's neck and pressed against this intense, white-hot pain as I fell to the ground, writhing in agony. My fifteen-year-old self had no idea that a pain so awful could exist. And in that moment, I naively thought that Charlie only nicked me a little with the box cutter.

But to my horror, that blade took a slice out of the left side of my chest, ripping through the tissue in between my ribs, beneath the left pectoral muscle but just above my stomach. My hands were covered in dark red blood, and as I looked into the gaping hole in my chest, I saw my subcutaneous fat cells and muscles, pulsating with every rapid beat of my heart.

"I need y'all to get me to a hospital," I screamed at the top of my lungs with my hands clutching my chest. I cried out: "I need to get stitches! Now!"

They say that God takes care of fools and babes, for which I am grateful because, in a stroke of good fortune, my friend Lisa was one of the girls on the scene.

Lisa's mom was a registered nurse, so Lisa immediately sprang into action and took me up to their fourth-floor apartment. In another stroke of good fortune, Lisa's mom just happened to be home, and she immediately began triaging my wound—keeping it clean and covered— as we waited for the ambulance to arrive. The EMTs seemed to take forever to get there, and my blood soaked through at least ten of Lisa's mom's towels as we waited.

As her mom tended to me, Lisa paged Rick,[129] with the code 911. Within minutes, both Rick and Max were at my side (like they always were in those days) just as the ambulance finally showed up. The EMTs placed an oxygen mask over my face, and the air from that mask felt like a blast of the purest, most refreshing air I'd ever breathed. It was a welcome relief from the humidity of that late August day, and I cherished every molecule of that delicious oxygen as the ambulance sped through the busy Brooklyn streets.

"Do you think I'm gonna need surgery," I asked Rick, filled with fear.

"Kid—you have a HOLE in you," he replied. "They gonna have to sew you up. But keep talking to me, man. We can't have you fall asleep."

The doctors didn't put me under as they sewed me up, opting instead for local anesthesia as they went to work putting me back together. I watched as they sutured my torn body like someone sewing up a hole in fabric, and then winced as they closed my chest with more than thirty staples—plunging the metal, one by one, into my skin with a staple gun. Despite the anesthetic, each shot of that staple gun pierced my skin with awesome ferocity, adding to my pain. When the procedure was finished, it looked like I had a zipper in my chest. I remember being surprised that I didn't need a blood transfusion despite losing so much blood in the slashing.

"You're lucky to be alive," the lead doctor told me after they were finished patching me up. "He got you right between the spleen, heart, and lungs. If that blade were just a centimeter higher or lower, you would be gone. You would have bled to death on that sidewalk. That kid is no friend of yours."

Just one centimeter higher or lower. Although my memory of that doctor's face faded away long ago, I can still hear the sound of his voice.

"If that blade were just a centimeter higher or lower…"

---

[129] Pagers, also known as beepers, were communication devices popular from the 1970s through the 1990s. They were primarily used to receive short messages or alerts.

I carry a permanent scar on my chest, but I barely even see it these days when I look at myself, shirtless in the mirror. Yet every now and then, when life blesses me with a special moment in my career or personal life—I reflect on that fateful August day. I thought of it on my wedding day, and after the birth of each of my three children because they all came within a centimeter of not existing. I thought of how close I'd come to dying nearly thirty years later, as I sat onstage with NBA legend Steph Curry, interviewing him one-on-one in front of hundreds of people about pay equity for women and creating opportunities for minority entrepreneurs.

And I thought of my near-tragedy a short while after that Curry talk, when I sat at a boardroom table directly next to former U.S. Secretary of State Condoleezza Rice as she discussed the Israel-Hamas War in a roomful of government leaders and corporate executives, with me being one of them. Little 'ole me from the hood with a seat at the table next to all these important people, discussing a geopolitical crisis. Just one centimeter higher or lower and none of it would have ever happened.

And then my mind inevitably turns toward Rick and Max, my brothers who were with me in that ambulance. My Day Ones. While I've been fortunate to soar towards higher heights in the years since—thanks to more than a few lucky breaks and help along the way— life hasn't been as kind to them.

The three of us started off at the same, humble level, raised in the same family. Born into adversity. We came up in Clinton Hill, Brooklyn in the late 1980s and 1990s, long before the gentrifying invaders showed up. This was the height of the crack era in New York, and in my mind, I can still see the empty crack vials littered on sidewalks, and beautiful tree-lined city blocks blighted by abandoned buildings, stray dogs, and addicts breaking into cars to steal radios.

As the three of us came of age, our father wasn't in the picture day-to-day, and our mom and grandmother did the very best they could to fill that gaping hole in our lives. But children need their father, and we were three boys who began to run wild during our adolescent years. Rick, who is two years older than me, was my hero back then. He was one of the best basketball players in our neighborhood, a scoring point guard who earned the nickname Special K—in homage to his hero, the New York City legend Kenny Anderson. Rick was so nice on the basketball court that a young designer from Fila who lived in our hood once gifted him a pair of exclusive kicks to model as he went from park to park destroying dudes.

Rick had an effortless swagger about him, and he always looked out for me. He used to let me rock his sneakers and sweatshirts to school now and then. I felt like I was the MAN whenever I wore Rick's stuff. On days that I got to wear his sneakers, it was like my bookish nerdiness and teenaged gawkiness disappeared, and were suddenly replaced by a cool, swaggering cockiness.

In my heart of hearts, I believe that if Rick had been born into a different family, with a father around every day to stick a foot in his ass, show him the right way of doing things and keep him on track—Rick would've made it to the NBA. That's how good he was.

And then there's my baby brother Max. Three years my junior, Max was blessed with our father's good looks. He also had a fiery temper and routinely got into fights at school and around the neighborhood. Our father was the only person on earth that Max would listen to, but Dad was never around when we were growing up. So, Max ran wild. Always in trouble in school and always gave Mom headaches with his incorrigible behavior. Max and I used to spar with each other damn near every other day, but because I was bigger than him, I used to get the best of him in those exchanges. During our battles, I would imagine myself to be a pro wrestler like Brett Hart or the Ultimate Warrior, and I'd always end our bouts by putting him in the sharpshooter[130] submission hold or catching him with

---

[130] The Sharpshooter is a professional wrestling submission hold, famously associated with Bret "The Hitman" Hart. It is one of the most iconic submission maneuvers in wrestling history.

a belly-to-belly suplex.[131] My size was the only reason why I'd win those bouts back then. That changed when he got older and stronger though. When we weren't fighting, Max was my shadow, following me everywhere I went.

When I was still in middle school, I'd bring Max along sometimes for my bike-riding adventures. It'd be me on my 10-speed and Max on the sweet orange BMX that Mom got him for Christmas one year. Max's BMX was the envy of the neighborhood.

Back in the summer of '94, Spike Lee was in our hood filming the movie *Clockers*, and we'd hopped on our bikes to go check out the movie set near the intersection of Fulton and Ashland Place. As we rode past Brooklyn Tech High School, an older thug—who was probably around eighteen or so—sped towards us on his bike and yelled out: "Ay, yo, shortie—gimme that MF bike."

Like a lion chasing a gazelle on the African savanna, that thug chased after my brother, and I was powerless to defend him. And out of a sense of fear and survival, my instinct was to let the thug take my little brother's bike. Mom could always get him another one, I figured. I was unable to protect Max, then. And I wouldn't be able to protect him from future traumas, either.

In the years after my slashing, Rick, Max, and I began our slow drift apart, with life taking us in different directions—to the point where we'd one day have little to do with each other—going months, and sometimes even years, without speaking. Despite his prodigious basketball talents, Rick never finished high school. Ever the resourceful hustler though, Rick always managed to keep some sort of job and was never without a little cash in his pocket.

Little Max started running with the wrong crowd and dropped out of school as well, although he was smart enough to get his GED

---

[131] A belly-to-belly suplex is a professional wrestling move, particularly a type of suplex, where one wrestler throws their opponent over their head using a powerful, explosive motion. This move is known for its impressive display of strength and technique.

at 17. Despite rarely setting foot in a high school classroom, Max passed that test in just one attempt.

As for me, nearly losing my life in the blink of an eye scared me into a stupor. I sleepwalked through the next year of high school, flunking off the basketball team and driving my poor mother to further worry and frustration with my aimlessness. Twenty-five years later, a therapist told me I was probably suffering from post-traumatic stress at the time.

But eventually, I started to get it together. While my brothers were still finding their way, I was hitting the books, and two years after the slashing I was on track for an academic scholarship.

The Burden Of The Black Bourgeoisie

"Then the LORD said to Cain, "Where is your brother Abel?"
"I don't know," he replied. "Am I my brother's keeper?""

—Genesis 4:9

Let's fast-forward ten years after that near-tragedy on Washington Ave. in Brooklyn. My brothers and I used to be as thick as thieves, but now we have little in common and are no longer as close as we once were. There was no falling out, but we're settling into the lives that we'll live as grown men. Socially, we are now moving in entirely different worlds. And economically, we're on divergent paths.

I'm about to graduate from college and am wrapping up my second summer as an intern on the news desk at Bloomberg News. I'm a strong candidate for a job as a reporter at three of the top news agencies in the country at this time. I'm brimming with confidence, and I see a bright future laid out in front of me. And while I'm making some good money as a Bloomberg intern, there's a huge raise from a competing news agency coming my way shortly.

My social circle no longer includes my brothers or the neighborhood crew I used to run with. Instead, I'm hanging out these days with young men and women who are like me. All about to graduate from college and focused on taking over the world. Partying every other night to burn off steam but hustling like hell during the daytime to build the lives we've always dreamed of.

On the flip side, my older brother Rick is still trying to find his way. He made a passing attempt at community college once but didn't finish. He still hasn't figured out how to make a steady living. He's often short on cash now that he's got to keep a roof over his head. Seeing the dude who used to be my hero starts to become a drag because whenever he's around I know the inevitable is coming.

"Ay yo, Jus, can you do me a favor," he'll ask. And then there'll be a request for money that he may or may not pay back. And out of a sense of obligation, I'll give it to him.

Little Max is even worse off. Even though he's got that GED, Max gravitated to the streets, and he's now on a journey that will see him venture in and out of jail more times than I can count over the next fifteen years. While we all gathered around Mom's Thanksgiving table the year I graduated, Max was spending his holiday in a jail cell on Riker's Island over an assault charge. As everyone enjoys their meal, and wonders why Max isn't there with us, I am secretly working with a bail bondsman to get him out. And like Rick, Max hits me up for cash damn near every time I see him, too. Out of that same sense of obligation, I'll give it to him, every single time. No questions asked.

My two brothers, the dudes who were once my best friends in another life, who were with me in that ambulance on the day my life nearly ended, are gradually becoming a burden. Because there's now a financial and psychological cost to being related to them.

As my career got underway, I was getting a taste of the Black middle-class struggle—finding myself caught between two worlds. On one end, I'm trying to find my way in corporate spaces and figure out how to fit into a new social dynamic where I'm now a "lonely only." And then on the other end, I have two brothers who are beginning to look to me as a financial safety net, which strains the close relationship we once had.

Deep down I know I'm no angel and that I'm no different than Rick and Max. I've been lucky more times than I can count. Like the time I nearly got kicked out of college during my freshman year for participating in an on-campus brawl. If it weren't for the big check that Uncle Juan wrote to the school, there would be no Bloomberg internship. No career on the horizon. No prospects. As I began my professional ascent, however, Rick and Max became my version of the Black Tax.[132] Yes, I've grinded my way to the top, putting in countless hours studying, preparing, and taking care of business. And I've put in that work alone. Yet, I harbor a profound sense of sadness over my good fortune in climbing my way out, while my brothers remain caught in the riptide of the myriad systemic issues that throw so many young Black men off track. To ward off that sadness, I throw a few dollars my brothers' way whenever they ask. And every time I see them, I wonder to myself, "How the hell did I make it while they didn't?"

Although I am trying to start on a path towards growing wealth for myself and snagging my piece of the so-called American Dream, I'm also becoming like the many middle-class Black Americans that Pew Research says are more likely than other groups to face the

---

[132] In one context, the term "black tax" refers to the financial burden that some Black individuals, particularly in African and African diaspora communities, feel as a result of providing financial support to their extended family members. This practice is common in cultures where communal support and obligation to one's family or community are strong. On the other hand, Shawn Rochester, author of The Black Tax: The Cost of Being Black in America, defines the "Black tax" as the financial cost imposed on Black Americans due to systemic racism and economic discrimination. According to Rochester, this "tax" manifests in various ways that significantly reduce the economic opportunities, income, wealth, and overall financial well-being of Black individuals and families.

added burden of giving or lending to family members in need.[133] The growing divide between my brothers and me mirrors the wealth divide that we see within Black America.

Removing sports and entertainment from the equation, Black people today are succeeding in finance, politics, public service, and business like never before in American history. Black Americans are also seeing greater gains in wages, wealth, and employment right now than at any point in recent memory.[134] And on the absolute high end? We're killing it. We've put a Black family in the White House (TWICE) and as of 2023 had eight Black CEOs running Fortune 500 companies, the highest total at any given time since that list was first published in 1955. There's no doubt that if you've got your proverbial act together, plus the right resources and connections—there's never been a better time than now to be young, talented, and Black.

But despite these obvious bright spots, there are far too many of us still falling behind. Black children today are three times more likely than White children to live in poverty.[135] One out of every three Black boys born today can expect to go to prison at some point during his lifetime.[136] We've lived out this data point in my family because there were three of us boys and little Max was the one to spend time in prison. So, yes, despite all the gains I just mentioned, the racial wealth gap continues to widen, and 20 percent of Black families have a negative net worth.[137] Black unemployment is also

---

[133] Source – Pew Research: "Extended Family Support and Household Balance Sheets." March 2, 2016

[134] Sources - National Community Reinvestment Coalition: "A Strong Black Economy Still Mired In Inequality: Race, Jobs And The Economy Update For January 2024. Additionally, Brookings Institute: "Black wealth is increasing, but so is the racial wealth gap." Jan. 9, 2024.

[135] Source – Center on Poverty & Social Policy at Columbia University: "The Black-White child poverty gap exists. Can we close it?" March 10, 2024

[136] Source: Tufts University Prison Divestment, 2024

[137] Source – US Department of the Treasury: "Racial Differences in Economic Security: The Racial Wealth Gap." Sept. 15, 2022

consistently twice that of White unemployment.[138] My brothers and I are flesh and blood examples behind this data, with each of us living some version of it in our day-to-day lives.

Ten years after the slashing, I find myself afflicted with a mean case of psychological whiplash. As I prepared to enter the corporate world full-time as a freshly minted graduate, I was getting a glimpse of what opportunity looks like, and just how beautiful life in this country can be when you're making good money and can enjoy the material comfort that comes with success. But this light illuminates the shadow of my past. In reality, I am slowly leaving behind the two people who meant more to me than anyone in the world during the growing-up stage of my life. Many years would pass before I'd figure out how to manage this growing divide with my brothers in a way that preserves my mental health.

No Man Left Behind

> *"Survivor guilt is a thief of joy—yet another secondary loss from death."*
>
> —Sheryl Sandberg

Survivor's guilt is an affliction of the mind that affects people who've survived a tragic event or traumatic circumstances when others have not. It's a condition that's been seen in people who've survived Nazi concentration camps[139] and soldiers who've survived wars.[140] It afflicted AIDS sufferers[141] who survived the early years of the

---

[138] Source - Pew Research Center: "Black unemployment rate is consistently twice that of whites." Aug. 21, 2013

[139] Source – United Nations: "I feel guilty I survived;' youngest Schindler's list Holocaust survivor tells United Nations her story." Jan. 31, 2018

[140] Source – Focus Marines Foundation: "Survivor's Guilt." 2024

[141] Source – NBC News: "Forty years after first documented AIDS cases, survivors reckon with 'dichotomy of feelings.'" June 5, 2021

epidemic as they watched their contemporaries die en masse, and it has marred students who miraculously walked away from school shootings unscathed.[142]

Within a corporate context, people who've escaped mass layoffs with their jobs intact have reported feelings of guilt and remorse after seeing colleagues let go.[143] On a personal front, I've felt the sting of survivor's guilt as I've advanced towards success in life while my brothers have struggled to find their way.

Stephen Joseph, a psychologist at the University of Warwick, has studied survivor's guilt extensively. In a study of the two hundred and sixty-six survivors of the 1987 capsizing of the MS Herald of Free Enterprise—a Belgian ferry—Joseph found sixty percent were afflicted with survivor's guilt. In his study, Joseph notes there were three types of survivors from this ordeal, including:

1. Those who felt guilty about remaining alive while others died.
2. Those who felt guilty about the things they failed to do.
3. Those who felt guilty about what they did to survive.

Looking back on the circumstances we came of age in, I see parallels to being stuck aboard a sinking ship. We were three Black boys being raised in a single-parent home, which meant that we were three-and-a-half times more likely to be poor as adults.[144] We are products of New York City's failing public schools of that era, with only one out of the three of us graduating from high school. And we came of age in a mixed bag of a neighborhood, where some families were materially well off, while others subsisted just above the

---

[142] Source – NBC Today.com "'I'm sorry I let you die': After a school shooting, children struggle with survivor's guilt.'" Jan. 17, 2023
[143] Source – Career Minds: "How to Manage Layoff Survivor Guilt." March 6, 2024
[144] Source – Instiute for Family Studies: "Less Poverty, Less Prison, More College: What Two Parents Mean For Black and White Children." June 17, 2021

poverty line. Research now confirms that the neighborhood where a child grows up has a profound impact on how their life turns out, [145] leaving me to wonder where little Max would be right now if he had the good fortune of being born and raised in a different environment.

Looking beyond my own household and not counting my brothers, I did an informal survey of ten Black males that I grew up with and spent significant time with over a ten-plus-year period. Three died before the age of 45, with two lost to violence and one to illness. Two served long, multi-year stints in prison. Two wound up living in poverty as adults, and three grew up to become reasonably successful by conventional standards. Just three successes out of ten of us. Of the three Black boys who grew up in my home, only one emerged with what is considered the conventional definition of success.

Like the survivors of the capsized MS Herald of Free Enterprise, I struggled for a long time with the question of why I made it out while others didn't. While I didn't feel the same sense of guilt that the survivors of that tragedy felt, I carried a burden of sadness at not being able to lift my brothers up.

Shaking Off The Burden Of Thriver's Guilt

> *"I want to thank me for believing in me. I want to thank me*
> *for doing all this hard work. I wanna thank me*
> *for having no days off."*
>
> —Snoop Dogg

Let's fast-forward another fifteen years.

Today, thanks to decades of hard work—and some fortuitous help along the way— my family and I are blessed to live in a beautiful home in a bucolic suburb of New York City. We live in a diverse community that includes a bevy of high-achieving Black

---

[145] Source – PublicSource: "How the neighborhood you grow up in affects your future."

professionals and enjoy a social circle that includes lawyers, doctors, bankers, entrepreneurs, and leaders in the worlds of academia and public service. My children are active participants in our local Jack and Jill[146] chapter and I find myself chuckling sometimes over how different their childhood is from mine. For example, the only wildlife that I saw growing up were lice-ridden swallows, pigeons, rats, stray dogs, and city squirrels.

My kids, on the other hand, live near a nature preserve and see blue jays and cardinals flying around our spacious backyard. Deer and rabbits occasionally show up in our yard as well. They're beautiful, but a pain because they like to munch on the plants in my beloved garden.

I make it a habit to count our blessings, knowing full well where I came from and how precarious our position in the middle class truly is. Because even as I allow myself to exhale and accept what hard work has provided for my family, I must also prepare for the rainy days that life can throw your way at any given moment. I've got to make sure we have enough to withstand the unexpected. Job loss. Illness. Disasters. Or worse.

No, I am not morbid. But as a provider, I must be there as a safety net for my wife and three children and, for my aging mother. This is my responsibility as a man. It is a responsibility that I embrace. But it is also a heavy weight to carry. So, with all this in mind, I now feel zero guilt in allowing myself to enjoy the things I've worked for. I've also freed myself from the burden of believing that it's my

---

[146] Jack and Jill of America, Inc. is a national organization founded in 1938 by Marion Stubbs Thomas in Philadelphia, Pennsylvania. It was established as a social organization for African American children, aiming to bring together children in a social and cultural environment. It focuses on leadership development, volunteer service, philanthropic giving, and educational programming. Jack and Jill is also made up of mothers who are committed to nurturing and strengthening children, ages 2 to 19. It has chapters across the country. I wish more Black children had access to it.

responsibility to carry others. Even my brothers, who rode with me in that ambulance long ago.

This freedom of conscience stems in large part from a hard lesson that I was forced to learn midway through my career about the difference between providing help to those in need versus becoming an enabler of bad habits and poor decision-making.

Several years ago, I was under the gun at work in a big way. I was on the hook to deliver a major year-in-review presentation to a roomful of senior executives that included a CEO and several board members. We were late on this project and we were already in the fourth quarter of the fiscal year. I blocked off my calendar the morning before the presentation to do a final review of my slides and rehearse my narrative, which included practicing answers to the tough questions I was expecting. A lot was riding on this presentation because a poor business review could derail the next year's strategy, negatively impact my bonus, and set up a roadblock on my path toward a promotion. But if I crushed it? The sky was the limit. But instead of singularly focusing on the task at hand, I made the mistake of answering the phone that morning when one of my brothers called. [147]

Although my brother had a job, he was behind on his rent by three months, and if he didn't pay it back in full by noon that day, he'd be evicted from his apartment with nowhere to go. Getting the money to him wouldn't be simple either because he didn't have a bank account, which meant I couldn't just send him the money quickly through Zelle or Venmo. (This was also in the days before those apps even existed.)

Allowing him to get evicted just wasn't an option for me, so I took precious time that should've been spent focusing on work to hustle down to Western Union to wire him the funds.[148] In addition

---

[147] I won't say which brother here.
[148] This was prior to Western Union launching an app that would speed up this type of transaction.

to putting a massive dent in my family's monthly budget (which I'd have to explain to my wife), this was a major distraction that could have derailed my immediate professional future. I knew that I couldn't allow this to happen again.

These types of asks from my brother were a regular occurrence, and because of how I'd handled them earlier in my career, they persisted and happened so many times I lost count. Over the years, I also found myself wasting too much valuable time—and even my peace of mind—on the affairs of others. I soon recognized that this was too high of a price to pay. Although I've still got a limitless heart when it comes to generosity to loved ones, I've set boundaries around personal loans and bailouts. Today, I generally try to avoid mixing money and family because it's damaged cherished relationships far too often for me.

I've also accepted the harsh truth that while now and then everyone needs a helping hand, we're also the products of our choices. I've made some good choices along the way, and I make no apologies for that.

CHAPTER ELEVEN

LEANING INTO FAITH

*"Sometimes you just got to have a little faith.
How else you think them White boys took over the world?"*

—Uncle G.

For the first nine years of my career, fear was my daily companion. It tucked itself within my blue Herschel bag—somewhere between the notebooks and pens and hitched a ride with me into the office during my commute. Monday through Friday, it was there. And it was there on weekends sometimes, too, during those free moments when my mind drifted back to my job and the week ahead. Fear took up a permanent residence in my mind. And it fed me a steady diet of negative thoughts that played on a running loop.

- "They're all skeptical of you, man. Just like them Reuters people."
- "You don't really belong here."
- "You're too large and too loud and too Black for corporate America, dude."
- "You're too 'hood for this place, my guy."

- "Maybe they're right to be skeptical of you, man."
- "You're a fucking imposter, bruh—straight up."

It's impossible to do your best work when you're afraid all the time. Fear is a great destroyer of peace. It'll have you looking over your shoulder and running from a bogeyman who doesn't exist. Fear will warp your mind and cloud your vision so that you see the world through a foggy lens. Fear will fool you into thinking everyone is out to get you. And as fear takes root in your mind, it will eat away at your body. Slowly, but surely, fear will destroy you from the inside out. One cell at a time.

It's easy to be afraid as a Black man in the United States. It's just as easy to be afraid if you're a Black man working in a White space like corporate America. Because these aren't always the most welcoming of places if you're a person of color, there's nothing irrational about being afraid of spaces where you don't feel welcome.

We're not born scared. We enter this world free, with the timeless sparkle of celestial starlight in our eyes. But this society of ours has an insidious way of making us afraid and snuffing out the starlight we're born with. Sometimes a little fear is a good thing. It's nature's way of alerting us to immediate danger and the threat of harm. And when this happens our heart rate speeds up, and our adrenaline shifts into gear to ensure we're on high alert and ready to flee. Within this context of fight or flight, fear is a survival mechanism. It's designed to be temporary. That's a good kind of fear because it can keep you alive.

The type of fear that I dragged with me into the office is the bad kind of fear. I feared that people were conspiring against me when I went to work every day. Unlike the temporary kind of fear that's designed to keep you alive, this fear existed in my head and was with me day in and day out. It didn't save me from any life-threatening dangers. Instead, it limited my creativity and kept me from being at my best.

This bad type of fear is contagious. Like a virus, it infects us through the images we're fed and stories we're told. We learned this fear from our elders, who had good reasons to be afraid of White spaces. I think back to the fear in ole Deacon John's voice during a Bible study when he said in his syrupy southern drawl: "Naw, suh, I don't fool with White people." I saw that same fear in my father's eyes when he dropped me off at a corporate golf event at a New Jersey country club during my Reuters days. (I never saw someone speed out of a parking lot so fast!)

My Mom didn't want me to be afraid of White spaces, so just like the show *Everybody Hates Chris*,[149] she sent me to a predominantly White middle school. I cried like a baby when she decided not to send me to the neighborhood school with my friends, but years later she told me: "I needed you to know how to socialize with them. To be friends with them. To be comfortable with them because I knew that these were the people who you were going to work with one day."

As a teenager, I saw the celestial starlight gradually grow dimmer in my friend Kevin's[150] eyes, leading him to drop out of high school and the sometimes-emasculating straight path to an entry-level career as a dime bag hustler. "You a Bryant Gumbel-ass nigga," he'd sometimes tease me when we'd hang out in the courtyard of our Brooklyn apartment complex, back when it was becoming clear that we were drifting apart. Kevin had as much charisma and mathematical talent as any young captain of industry. While I went on to finish school and start my career, Kev advanced from being a dime-bag hustler into a major player in the drug game. The year I was promoted to

---

[149] *Everybody Hates Chris* is a sitcom inspired by the childhood of comedian Chris Rock. It aired from 2005 to 2009 and humorously depicts the challenges Chris faces growing up in Brooklyn during the 1980s. Chris, the main character, attends an all-white school called Corleone Junior High, where he often feels out of place. His school experience is marked by bullying, racial discrimination, and awkward social interactions.

[150] This is a pseudonym to protect my old friend's identity.

executive director at JPMorgan Chase, Kev was sentenced to thirty years to life in prison for operating the largest fentanyl ring on the East Coast.

Through some minor miracle, the starlight never dimmed in my eyes. While friends like my man Kev were on the block hustling, I was hitting the books and focusing on school. But we were all afraid of being in White spaces. That fear kept many of my friends from even trying to play the game I was playing. And I brought that fear we all shared with me into the corporate world.

Fortunately for me though, by 2015, my fear had finally faded a bit. I'd found a nice groove at Fidelity, which was the first large corporation where I felt fully at home. I was killing it from a performance standpoint, my manager was cool as hell, the comp was solid, and I'd become good friends with my mostly White, New England-based colleagues. We were a team who genuinely enjoyed working with each other.

And as corny and naïve as it may sound now—more than a decade into the MAGA movement— the Obama effect also played a role in my fear fading away. My Fidelity years coincided with the second White House term of a Black president whose middle name was Hussein. Surely, times were changing, right? Because in White spaces like New Hampshire and Vermont, and Iowa and Oregon, and Maine and Washington state—places with tiny populations of Black and other people of color—Obama had won decisively. Not just once. But twice. By substantial margins. So, in my naïve thinking, I figured, if millions of White people can accept a man like Barack as their president TWICE, then surely, they can accept a guy like me as their colleague or boss in a corporate office, right? Suddenly, the White space of corporate America didn't seem so scary for a large, loud Black man like me anymore.

Before Obama won the White House, the idea of a Black person occupying the ultimate White space was so unrealistic that it was a recurring trope in Black comedy. From Cedric the Entertainer's hilarious riff on why a Black man couldn't handle the presidency in the *Original Kings of Comedy*, to the Chris Rock film *Head of State*, and Dave Chappelle's famous 2004 comedy sketch imagining a Black George W. Bush, the idea of a Black American ever holding the presidency was an outlandish theme that comedians once got a lot of mileage out of. America was too racist to ever let such a thing happen.

Only, suddenly, that comedic trope wasn't so funny anymore, because, for a moment in time, it seemed like King's Dream had come true. If you wanted a job, even the biggest, most important job in the world, you just needed to be the best person for it, no matter your skin tone, hair texture, or gender. The door was no longer closed to any opportunity if you were Black. You just needed the skills and confidence to go for it. Plus a few connections. (That always helps.) The Obama years gave me that. The Obama years gave many Black Americans that. Those years gave us the illusion that the Dream had been realized.[151]

The Obama years overlapped with one of the most dangerous times in my career. I'd finally found a comfort zone. I was less afraid back then because my job had become easy, and I envisioned myself sitting in that role for the next twenty-five years and getting fat and happy off my generous comp and benefits—which included a ridiculous 100% match on my 401(k) contributions up to seven percent.[152] Plus, I was in a White space where I felt safe. I never thought such a place could exist in the corporate world. It wouldn't be so easy to give up.

---

[151] I am referring to Dr. Martin Luther King Jr.'s dream, where we'd live in a nation where racial harmony and equality are realized, where segregation and discrimination are abolished, and where freedom and justice prevail for all Americans.

[152] This is unheard of! The sweetest benefits package I've ever enjoyed.

The Corporate Comfort Trap

"A comfort zone is a beautiful place, but nothing ever grows there."

—Gina Milicia, photographer.

"Comfort zones are where dreams go to die."

—Regina King, actress.

By June 2015, I wanted to lean into that Fidelity life forever. Anika and I had just uprooted our family from a duplex in tony Cobble Hill, Brooklyn to a handsome four-bedroom Tudor in South Orange, NJ, and she'd given birth to our son only a month before the move. Between moving to a new house and bringing a second child into our family, the last thing I wanted at that time was another massive change in my life. I wanted a comfort zone. It'd taken me more than a decade to find a cushy spot where I fit in socially and could coast professionally, and I had zero interest in ever giving that up. At the time, I would've been just fine with my internal communications job at Fidelity being the pinnacle of my professional life because I'd finally found a White space of which I wasn't afraid.

Never mind that I had other untapped talents just sitting there, BEGGING to be taken off the shelf and developed. During that phase of my life and career, comfort was my focus.

I lacked the foresight to envision who I'd become if I stayed in that job for as long as I'd intended. I couldn't see that had I remained on the Fidelity path, one day I'd be an old man, nearing the end of my life, wondering where all the time went and why I didn't try harder to make a bigger impact on the world using the talents I'd been given. I couldn't see from the eyes of my future self, all that I'd regret if I didn't chase my dreams and instead limited myself to a job that would never push me to live up to my fullest potential.

After all those years of being scared all the time, easy is what I wanted, and Fidelity WAS EASY. I daydreamed about working there until I was sixty-five and then riding off into the sunset with the stacks of cash I would've tucked away during my decades of blissful toil.

But a career, much like a human life, is a long, winding journey with twists, turns, and fork-in-the-road moments. Red pill or blue pill moments.[153] Pivotal moments when you can decide to either stick with what's easy, comfortable, and familiar or venture off into the unknown for something new with more upside.

Fork-in-the-road moments have a funny way of presenting themselves to you in times when you're not looking for them. I was lounging by the pool on a warm, late June morning when I got an innocuous LinkedIn note from a recruiter about a job leading digital strategy for a mid-sized mutual fund company.

"Hey babe, I think I'm going to flirt with these people just for the hell of it," I said to Anika as we soaked up some sun. "I ain't tryin' to leave Fido, but lemme at least see what they're talking about. This looks kinda interesting. And who knows, maybe the pay is on point."

Nothing Ventured, Nothing Gained.

"A ship in harbor is safe, but that is not what ships are built for."

—John A. Shedd, author.

In the film and novel *Life of Pi*, both Pi and his tiger pal Richard Parker find themselves stranded on a lifeboat in the middle of the Pacific Ocean. For an unimaginably long time, they drift throughout the Pacific, enduring brutal storms, terrifying waves, and searing, relentless heat.

---

[153] The "red pill or blue pill" choice comes from the 1999 film *The Matrix*. In a key scene, the protagonist, Neo, is offered two pills by Morpheus, a mentor figure. The choice between the two pills symbolizes the decision between confronting a harsh truth or remaining in comfortable ignorance.

At their most desperate moment—just when it seems they're on the brink of dying from starvation, thirst, or exposure—they miraculously land on a lush green island. This island has all the food they'll ever need and freshwater ponds for them to drink from. For a moment, Pi is tempted to stay on this island forever, rather than traverse the endless Pacific again in search of civilization.

But despite the appearance of safety, Pi notices something's off about this island. There's no wildlife on it like birds or insects. At night, the plants release an acid that digests any living thing on the ground. To his horror, Pi realizes that the island is carnivorous and that if he and Richard Parker stay there any longer, they'll be eaten alive. If they're to survive, they'll need to leave this illusory comfort zone—a place that in the long run will lead to an unimaginably painful death.

I'd endured my share of rough seas and harsh conditions during the early years of my career, and I certainly had no interest in walking away from my cushy little spot at Fidelity. It's okay to spend a little time in a comfort zone to get your bearings. I certainly needed one after a rough beginning to my career. But deep down I knew I was capable of more. I'd come into corporate America full of dreams and confidence and believing that bigger things were in store for me. I had even bigger dreams about the positive impact I could have on the community through my work. If I had stayed at Fidelity, those dreams would have been eaten alive. Fidelity had become my carnivorous island.

Six weeks after I replied to that recruiter's LinkedIn message expressing interest in the digital strategy role, I sat on the beach in Santa Monica, agonizing over what to do next. I'd gone through a series of interviews with senior leaders at what could be my new firm, including their Chief Marketing Officer, and had apparently blown them away. Not one of those senior leaders was a person of color but that didn't matter to me one bit. During those interviews, I imagined myself to be like President Obama—speaking within a

White space like the Senate or a White House press conference—filled with calm, poise, and charm.

I crushed that interview and they wanted to hire me so bad they offered me a substantial raise above what I'd been making at Fidelity. Tens of thousands more, in fact, along with an annual bonus that was more than triple my previous bonus rate.

Only then did my Fidelity friends—my WONDERFUL Fidelity friends—counter with an even bigger offer from a monetary standpoint. The only problem was that there was little professional growth in what I'd be doing on a day-to-day basis. Sure, they came correct on the money. Boy, did they ever come correct on the money! They also offered me the easier way out.

I was tempted to take Fidelity's money, along with that easy job. As I sat on the beach, the nasty old fear that used to live in my mind, came back for a visit. The fear was different this time. It wasn't a fear of a new White space in corporate America anymore. Instead, the fear told me that it'd be easier to go with the devil I knew rather than risk going for something greater with the unknown. Fear wanted me to stay within that dangerous comfort zone.

There were aspects to the new job opportunity that I'd never done before. I'd be in charge of the digital editorial experience for an entire company. I'd have to build a strategy to help their portfolio managers market both themselves and their products through cool, engaging digital content. I'd work directly with a senior leadership team that would regard me as an expert and I'd own the company's agency relationships. I'd work across their advertising and digital experience teams. This was a chance at real, professional growth.

But since I didn't have experience in every aspect of the job, I was afraid to take it. I was afraid the people at the new company would be cold and hostile. I worried I'd flame out quickly, get fired, and be stuck at square one with two kids and a mortgage hanging over my head. I was more afraid of what I might lose in taking the new opportunity rather than hopeful about all that I could gain by taking the next step in my career.

As I sat on the beach, agonizing, my fears were at war with my faith in the possibility of something better.

Never Be Afraid To Bet On Yourself

> "You will never do anything in this world without courage. It is the greatest quality of mind next to honor."
>
> —Aristotle.

> "The future belongs to risk-takers."
>
> —Brian Tracy,
> Canadian motivational speaker

When you're a kid, being curious and adventurous comes easy. You're not fully aware of all that you could lose by taking risks and going on fun adventures. And I was damn fearless as a kid, especially during my middle school summers in New York City. Back then, Mom couldn't afford to send both my younger brother and me to summer camp. So, while Max got shipped off to a day camp every day at a church in south Brooklyn, I had free rein to pretty much do as I pleased for the blissful nine weeks every summer between grades six and nine.

With only the single dollar or two that Mom would leave for me on her dresser in the morning, plus my trusty 10-speed bike, my man Kev and I used to link up like clockwork early in the day and make our rounds. On days when our adolescent appetites raged for more sustenance than quarter waters,[154] salt and vinegar chips, Now &

---

[154] A "quarter water" was a term used in Black neighborhoods, particularly in the Northeast U.S., to refer to a small, inexpensive fruit-flavored drink, often sold in small plastic bottles or pouches. The name "quarter water" comes from the fact that these drinks were traditionally sold for 25 cents (a quarter). They are typically known for their sweet taste and low cost, which made them popular where I'm from.

Laters,[155] and egg rolls from Ms. Lao's Chinese Restaurant, we'd sneak into the cafeteria on the Pratt Institute campus and steal cheeseburgers to fuel up for the day. On days like those, when our bellies were full, we'd be motivated to explore, and the entire city was our playground. With no bike helmets and weaving in and out of traffic, we'd sometimes ride our bikes through Brooklyn, over the Brooklyn Bridge, and all the way uptown to the north end of Central Park.

When we were bored, we'd play our version of a game called Manhunt, where we'd sneak into Pratt buildings and try to navigate our way to the rooftops without being seen by the security guards. On a couple of occasions, they spotted us, and then the chase would be on. But they never caught us. Those middle school summer days would drag on for what seemed like forever and the only thing on our agenda was finding some new heart-pounding adventure to get into.

More than twenty years later, as I sat on that Santa Monica beach wondering what to do next with my career, the adventurous child I once was couldn't have been more different than the fearful, risk-averse man I'd become.

Somewhere along the way during my journey to adulthood, I'd adopted (deep within the recesses of my subconscious mind) a scarcity mindset. I feared that opportunities for me were limited and that I'd be better off holding onto the little successes I'd achieved rather than searching for new frontiers to explore. The fearless child who'd ride his bike from Brooklyn to upper Manhattan in New York City traffic with no helmet had grown into a fearful man who'd lost his sense of exploration and adventure. I had become preoccupied by what I could lose and developed an almost paralyzing fear of failure.

---

[155] Now & Laters are a type of chewy candy known for their intense fruit flavors. They are rectangular, individually wrapped pieces that come in a variety of flavors, such as cherry, grape, apple, and watermelon.

Choosing A Path When You Reach A Fork In The Road

"If somebody offers you an amazing opportunity but you are not sure you can do it, say yes—then learn how to do it later!"

—Richard Branson,
founder of the Virgin Group

At the westernmost point on the island of Jamaica, in the town of Negril, there's a bar called Rick's Café. Rick's is located right on the edge of a cliff, and it's a place to hear cool local bands, do some people watching, and drink Flaming Bob Marleys—a delicious cocktail of grenadine, gallino, and green mint cream, topped off with flammable Bacardi 151 that's set on fire before you drink it. (Of course, you're supposed to blow out the fire before taking a sip.)

What's most memorable about Rick's though, are two things. First, you can see arguably the most beautiful sunsets in the entire world from that café. And second, Rick's is a place where thrill seekers come to cliff dive. At its highest point, divers can take the plunge from thirty-five feet in the air.

During a trip to Jamaica for a friend's wedding years ago, I stood at that bar, sipping on a Marley, and looking on in amazement as one-by-one, brave souls took the plunge. I was jealous of their fearlessness and how they could defiantly look death in the face and make a jump that would send a surge of adrenaline and excitement coursing through their bodies. I envied how these jumpers could tap into that feeling I once felt as an adventurous New York City kid. Most of all, I envied the faith these jumpers had in themselves. Despite my solid swimming abilities, I didn't have enough trust in myself to leap. I was good enough to do it but lacked the courage at the time.

The memory of myself on the sidelines at Rick's Café flooded my mind as I deliberated whether to seize this new opportunity. I tried to envision where I'd be professionally twenty years down the line if I stayed where I was versus where I'd be if I took the chance to expand my professional capabilities.

I decided I'd regret not jumping off the proverbial cliff and doing more with my career. And so as much as it pained me, I said goodbye to Fidelity, a stable company with great people where I could've spent the next two decades doing a job that paid well and had great benefits—but ultimately came with a limited upside. Walking away from a White space where I felt safe was one of the hardest decisions I ever made. But it would quickly become clear I'd made the right decision.

It's All A Confidence Game.

"I'm LeBron, baby. I can play on this level. I got some game."

—Barack Obama,
speaking on his political skills in 2004,
four years before he captured the White House.

After nearly twenty years in corporate America, I've developed a five-part formula for building professional confidence.

- First, you've got to be prepared. And I mean PREPARED—almost to the point of obsession.

- Secondly, you've got to put yourself in positions that will demand more from you than you think you're capable of. You need metaphorical mountains to climb and cliffs to dive from. Without big challenges like these, you'll never grow.

- Third, you've got to approach these mountains and cliffs with optimism. You'll never succeed without having deep, abiding faith that everything will work out. You've got to believe in yourself because if you don't believe in YOU, no one else will either.

- Fourth—you've got to crush whatever challenges come your way. When you climb those mountains and dive off those cliffs, you've got to succeed. Failure isn't an option …

BUT IF, by some off chance you do, in fact, fail—you've got to pick yourself up and try again. BE PERSISTENT. Take the lessons from any losses, make smart adjustments, and try and try again until you get it right. Once you conquer all four elements of this formula, you're going to feel like LeBron with a basketball in his hands. Nothing will be able to stop you.

My new job after Fidelity was that proverbial mountain for me to climb. It was my version of that cliff at Rick's Café. After leaping into the new role, it took me a few months to find my way. But once I did, it was ON. At times, I did feel like LeBron in that job. With every little success, those old fears receded. My sense of imposter syndrome disappeared. That nagging fear of White spaces. Gone. Gradually, my scarcity mindset gave way to an abundance mindset.[156] And I even reconnected with the adventurous kid that I used to be.

The portfolio managers I worked with—who picked stocks for mutual funds and exchange-traded funds that would earn investors billions of dollars—were relying on my expertise to convince financial advisors that their products were worth investing client money in. These brilliant financiers—these products of private schools, Ivy

---

[156] An abundance mindset is a psychological and philosophical approach where individuals believe that there are ample resources and opportunities available to everyone. People with an abundance mindset are characterized by:

- Optimism: They view the world as full of possibilities and opportunities, rather than limited and constrained.
- Generosity: They are more likely to share resources and support others, believing that doing so will not diminish their own opportunities.
- Collaboration: They prefer working together and seeing others' success as a positive aspect, rather than competing to outdo others.
- Growth-Oriented: They are open to learning, growth, and improvement, seeing challenges as opportunities to learn and expand.

In contrast, a scarcity mindset is based on the belief that resources are limited and that one person's gain is another's loss. Those with a scarcity mindset might feel more competitive, anxious, or threatened by others' successes. Adopting an abundance mindset can lead to greater creativity, collaboration, and overall satisfaction.

League universities, and country clubs had no idea with whom they were dealing. They didn't see the kid who'd worked his way up from nothing. They damn sure didn't see an imposter. They just saw before them a credible expert who they'd have to listen to if they wanted to succeed in getting people to buy what they were selling. My approach to the work earned me the backing of the Chief Investment Officer of the firm, and one senior executive even referred to me and a peer, a hotshot young White dude as the future of the company.

Eventually, I reached a comfort zone in that job and then a funny thing happened. I grew bored and began to set my sights on bigger opportunities with new challenges to conquer. The adventurer I once was had been reborn and the idea of sitting ensconced in a job for twenty-five years without trying something new sounded like torture. I was too confident for that now.

Forget Being Like Mike. Be Like JR Smith.

One of my best friends at that fund management firm lived in a beautiful waterfront apartment complex overlooking Manhattan from across the Hudson River in Weehawken, New Jersey. At the time, New York Knicks guard JR Smith was one of his neighbors. "We lived in the same building, bro. And sometimes I'd walk outside and see him smoking weed on his balcony," he told me. "He had two dope cars in the garage, and he used to throw the sickest parties."

As a Knicks fan, JR Smith drove me crazy. During his time in the NBA, he was what's known as an "irrational confidence guy." In basketball, an irrational confidence guy is a dude who has an overinflated level of belief in his shooting and scoring abilities. When he's on fire, his performance can lift a team to the highest of heights. But when he is off, the opposite happens, and he can quickly shoot your team out of a game. Even if he's ice-cold and missing, the irrational confidence guy will keep on shooting because he has a belief deep down that the next shot is going to go in. On nights when he was hot, JR was one of the most electrifying players in the NBA.

But when he was off, he was BAD. This is why I had a love/hate relationship with JR Smith during his time with the Knicks. Being an irrational confidence guy in basketball isn't always a good thing. But when you're a Black man who works in corporate America, being an irrational confidence guy is a necessity. Confidence is the armor that you must strap on to survive all the slings and arrows that will come your way.

Although I only spent three years at that fund management firm, those years transformed my career. During that time, I evolved from a scared, junior-level employee into an almost irrationally confident shot-caller who was ready for a bigger job. Like JR Smith's stupefying belief in himself on a basketball court, I believed in my ability to operate in a senior leadership capacity wherever I worked. That role consistently provided big enough challenges that enabled me to feel a real sense of accomplishment when I conquered them. For three years those successes snowballed, and each win bred more confidence.

Toward the end of my time there, my confidence grew to the point where I didn't fear White spaces anymore, even when they revealed themselves not to be so welcoming. I'll never forget what it was like in that office the day after Donald Trump shocked the world and captured the presidency. That morning, our CEO called it a great day for America. A portfolio manager who I was cool with and used to grab beers with from time to time told me with the brightest smile: "Man, THIS is the election where we decided to be proud of ourselves again." On our sales floor, I noticed that a bunch of my colleagues had placed those red "Make America Great Again" hats on their desks.

The day after that election I was in a state of shock, stunned that the numerous blatant instances of racism and sexism from Trump both before AND during that campaign weren't an automatic disqualifier in the minds of so many voters— especially the people I worked with. All that Trump support in my office served as a wake-up call for how unwelcoming corporate environments can be for people of color.

The night after the election, I needed a happy hour, so I went out for a beer with one of my buddies at the firm, a White dude. With serious eyes and in a sobering voice he said: "I'm telling you, Justin, there's still a lot of racism out there. You'd be surprised, man, but it's still there. The casual racism that people bring up in conversations these days is shocking. And in a bizarre, unmeasurable way, I think Trump gave people new license to be awful."

The aftermath of the 2016 election was bruising for a lot of us, but I'd discovered something about myself during that timeframe. My confidence had risen to the point where although I was surrounded by Trump lovers (and all that was implied by being a Trump supporter,) I wasn't the dude who feared White spaces anymore. I was no longer the guy who was afraid to take risks, either.

I was equipped with the armor of irrational confidence and faith in myself, and I wasn't about to allow a bunch of Trumpies to send me back down that rabbit hole of fear. And in the months following that election, I did some of my best work for that firm and positioned myself for something bigger and better in the years to come.

In the decade since then, Trumpism has further entrenched itself as a corrosive force in our society and there's no doubt that his movement still enjoys support in some corners of the corporate world—such as places like the sales floor at my old fund management firm.[1] We've also seen a significant backlash in recent years to the corporate-driven social justice movement following the murder of George Floyd.

Neither of these circumstances has dented my confidence in what's possible for Black talent in the corporate world. There has never been a better time than now to be alive if you're a Black American, and as long as you are prepared, ambitious, optimistic, and GOOD at what you do, the only limitations for your career are those that you place on yourself. This approach has carried me into the executive ranks of one of the world's largest banks and has opened doors for me that I couldn't have imagined earlier in my career. It's also left no doubt in my mind that even better days are ahead.

ACKNOWLEDGMENTS

In August 2022, *Company Men* was dead in the water—just another good idea that would never see the light of day as a full-grown project. I'd developed a proposal for this book in 2021 and spent the next year trying to convince publishers and literary agents why I thought it was worth investing in. That effort proved to be futile. They told me the marketplace didn't want this book so I put *Company Men* on the shelf, alongside many other great ideas that would never come to fruition. It was a dream deferred.

My family and I were vacationing at the time in beautiful Bethany Beach, Delaware, where I was spending my days hanging out at the beach, feasting on barbeque and seafood, and frantically refreshing my Twitter feed for days on end awaiting news that superstar Utah Jazz guard Donovan Mitchell was finally being traded to my beloved New York Knicks.[2] *Company Men* was the last thing on my mind. Then I got the call.

Charles Kim,[3] a literary agent specializing in BIPOC[4] writers in the United States, had gotten hold of my book proposal and wanted to work with me in finding a publisher who'd bring this book to market. He delivered a fiery pep talk for the ages during that phone call and breathed new life into the project. Before that

---

[1] That company was acquired in 2018 by a larger asset management firm.
[2] Donovan Mitchell was eventually traded … to the Cleveland Cavaliers.
[3] Charles Kim is also the co-founder and president of Third State Books, which specializes in Asian American authors.
[4] BIPOC stands for Black, Indigenous, and people of color.

phone call, my energy for this book had been fully exhausted, but Charles gave it a second life. Without Charles, *Company Men* would have never come to fruition. More than anything, I needed someone other than me who believed in it—and he did. Charles' belief gave me the extra jolt of energy that I needed to get this over the finish line.

I wish I could tell you that *Company Men* is solely the product of my own knowledge and expertise, but I'd be lying if I did. This book is a work of crowd-sourced wisdom, which I've quietly gathered from leaders and colleagues that I've worked with over the last twenty years. A few leaders stand out for me, and without them realizing it, their pearls of wisdom are sprinkled throughout these pages. From Tynnetta McIntosh and Byna Elliott, who challenged me with career-expanding opportunities, to leaders like Sekou Kaalund, Thasunda Brown-Duckett, Deb Langford, and Ahtis Davis, who showed me that it is indeed possible to be a trailblazing change agent in corporate America as a person of color.

I've also got to give a shout-out to my community, in particular the Suburb Bros crew of the Oranges in New Jersey. This distinguished group of highly accomplished Black men provided a sounding board for this project as well as a valuable source of interviews that helped me to tell this story. They helped me to articulate the challenges of walking the tightrope as a Black man in corporate America. Three of them, Jamison Antoine, Chad Bennett, and Clyde Lee, served as accountability partners and advisers, and their influence is on display throughout these pages. Suburb Bros Walter Douglas, Jr., Christopher Harvell, Monk Inyang, Arinze Onugha, and James Ward gave me so much of their time with in-depth interviews, while my mom, Patricia Grant, and my rock-star in-laws, Dr. Bonnie Thornton-Dill and Jack Schuler opened their homes to me as a writers' retreat. This book could never have happened without you. (Honorable mention to my main man Matt Gunn as well.) I appreciate you all.

www.ingramcontent.com/pod-product-compliance
Lightning Source LLC
Chambersburg PA
CBHW050256010526
44107CB00033B/1400/J